Madame Alexander
COLLECTOR'S DOLLS II
Second Series

by

Patricia R. Smith

EDITORS: Susan Rogers
Karen Penner

COVER: Cissy Ice Capade used for 20th Edition,
1960-1961 called "Tosca" from "Operama".

Published by:
COLLECTOR BOOKS
P.O. Box 3009
Paducah, Kentucky 42001

DEDICATION

Volume II is also dedicated to Madame Beatrice Alexander, the world is a more beautiful place because of her abilities and talents. Madame Alexander's dolls have filled the make-believe world of children and adults, and are a permanent part of our society, so will continue to give joy and beauty for all time.

Additional copies of this book may be ordered from:

COLLECTOR BOOKS
P.O. Box 3009
Paducah, Kentucky 42001

@$19.95 Add $1.00 for postage and handling.

Copyright: Patricia R. Smith, 1981
ISBN: 0-89145-145-5

Printed by IMAGE GRAPHICS, Paducah, Kentucky

CREDITS

A group of 219 color slides of Alexander dolls were sent to us to use, followed later by a registered letter asking us not to use them. We sent out a request for "help" through the leading national doll paper. The response was tremendous, and it was a joy to see how many collectors were willing to share their dolls and information. Our very, very special "thanks" go to these collectors.

Our special thanks to Marge Meisinger for loaning many of her catalogs, magazines and newspapers. Unless photo credits are listed, the photographs used were taken by the owner.

Nancy Arnott
Sue Austin
Jackie Barker
Lilah Beck: photos by Renie Culp
Gladys Brown
Barbara Boury: Photos by Lesley Richards
Mickey Canan: Photos by Dwight F. Smith
Ambri Cardenas
Bessie Carson: Photos by Dwight F. Smith
Janine Chatstrom
Donna Colopy
Karen Conlay
Sue Conners
Marlowe Cooper
Sandra Crane
Linda Crowsey: Photos by Jack Doherty
Renie Culp
Rita DiMare
LaDonna Dolan: Photos by Ted Long
Beth Donar
Dave & Kathy Ethington: Photos by Lee Welpley
Sandy Fleckenstein
Beth French: Photos by Dr. Deanne Bell
Pat Gardner: Photos by Dwight F. Smith
Susan Geotz
Martha Gragg
Betty Hazard: Photo by Lee Welpley
Bernice Heister
Elizabeth Henderson
Mildred Hightower: Photos by Cindy Hightower
Mimi Hiscox
Dianne Hoffman/Turn of Century Antiques
    1421 S. Broadway, Denver, Co.
    Photos by Steve Schweitberger
Joann Ide: Photos by Dave Ide
Sharon Ivy: Some photos by Dwight F. Smith
Roberta Jackson: Photos by Ted Long
Virginia Jones: Photos by Dwight F. Smith
Clarice Kemper
Sherry Kraft
Roberta Lago: Photos by Ted Long
Peggy Lewis: Photos by Dwight F. Smith
Maxine Look: Photos by Fay Rodolfos

Kathy Lyons
Margaret Mandel: Some photos by Dwight F. Smith
Barbra Jean Male: Photos by Michael Male
Barbara McKeon: Photos by Fay Rodolfos
Marge Meisinger
Mariann's Doll House (Billie McCabe):
    Photos by Dwight F. Smith
Rosemary Meyecic
Mrs. A. P. Miller
Jay Minter: Photos by Dwight F. Smith
Elizabeth & Rose Montesano: Photos by Isolde Jackson
Betty Motsinger
Florence Black Musich
Fannie Nedbalek: Photos by Dwight F. Smith
Carole Nori
Pam Ortman
Anita Pacey: Photos by Dwight F. Smith
Mary Partridge: Photos by Ted Long
Jaime Pendlebury: Photos by Chuck Pendlebury
Vita Pennington
Carrie Perkins: Photos by Ted Long
Lesley Richards
Nancy Roeder: Photos by Susan Deats
Doris Richardson
Shirley's Doll House, Wheeling, Ill.
Susan Rogers
Lillian Roth
Kathleen Rudisill
Paula Ryscik
Pat Sebastian
Barbara Schilde
Marion Schmuhl
Charmaine Shields
Deedee Shields
Pat Spirek
Helena Street
Ethel Stewart: Photos by Ted Long
Mary Sweeney
Marjorie Uhl
Mary Williams
Loramay Wilson
Glorya Woods
Judi Zemanek

FIRST LADY OF THE DOLL WORLD BEGINS NEW CAREER AT AGE 83

The above is the title of an article by John Platero in the "Lifestyle" section of *The Evening News*, Harrisburg, Pa. October 31, 1978. The following is that article.

Dateline: West Palm Beach, Fla. (AP) Madame Alexander, who has brought happiness to children round the world for over half a century with her exquisite line of dolls, has launched a new career at 83 . . . recorded stories for youngsters.

Although the more than 5,000 Alexander dolls she has created over the past 53 years have left her financially comfortable, the octogenarian's love for children remains insatiable. "Now I want to do with children's records what I did with dolls," she said.

In her first album, Madame Alexander narrates the fantasy world of dolls in a moving manner that tugs at the heartstrings of young and old alike.

"Have you ever watched how a little girl hugs a doll?" she asked. "She holds it tenderly and always carefully puts it down. That's the maternal instinct born in her and which she has seen in her mother."

Because of the vital role a doll has in helping a child mature, Madame Alexander has never made a mechanical doll. Instead, her creations emphasize detail down to the creases in the knuckles of the tiny fingers and the miniscule eyelashes like those of a baby.

"To allow a doll to perform mechanically for a child would have the tendency to have her sit back and have others perform for her," explained the woman who delights those near her with her enthusiasm.

She speaks often about her youth when, as the oldest of four girls, she watched her father, a German immigrant, struggle to make a living in New York City with his porcelain repair shop.

"I wasn't unhappy, and having to help care for my sisters was my first training to be an executive." she said. In those days, she had no doll of her own, but was allowed to play with the broken porcelain dolls that were brought to her father for repair.

"I saw so many children and unhappy parents who had broken dolls that I began to dream of making a doll that would not break," Madame Alexander recalled. In the 1920's, she designed and made her first cloth dolls which sold in her father's shop for $14.40 a dozen, or $1.98 each.

Today, these dolls are collector's items worth more than $300.00 each.

She soon convinced her husband, Philip Behrman, to quit his job with a New York hat company and take over the business end of the budding enterprise she had begun.

Inspired by literature, she gave life and faces to famous characters . . . Juliet, Sleeping Beauty, Cinderella, Scarlett O'Hara and Snow White to name only a few. And she made boy dolls as well, for example, Beau Brummel, David Copperfield and Butch McGuffey.

She also made "The Little Women" dolls early in her career. These were the four sisters in Louisa May Alcott's novel.

"There were no pictures in the book at that time, but the "Little Women" became a part of me because we were four girls in our family." she said.

Over the years, she has recreated in dolls many film stars and world personalities such as Queen Elizabeth II, Sonja Henie, Jacqueline Onassis and her daughter Caroline, Ginger Rogers and the wives of the first five Presidents, from Martha Washington to Louise Adams.

The question that has gone unanswered over the years by doll lovers was why she never made a Shirley Temple doll. Madame Alexander explained:

"I always thought Shirley Temple was extremely talented, but about the time she became a child star I had been quoted in a newspaper interview that I disapproved of commercializing on a child's efforts," she said "Because I couldn't go against what I had said, I did not make the doll."

She admits it hurt her financially at the time, but Madame Alexander has a strong moral character. "Buyers would come wanting 90 percent of their puchases in Shirley Temple dolls, but I just couldn't give in." she said.

It was the Dionne quintuplets that pulled her out of her financial doldrums that time. She was given permission by the Canadian government to see the five infants in the hospital where they were born. She added the Dionne girls to her doll line and it was an immediate success.

Now, Madame Alexander is semi-retired and a widow, and her business is run by her daughter and son-in-law, Mildred and Bill Birbaum, and her grandson, Alexander.

Her home is decorated with paintings and art objects. But some of her dolls are found in every room. When asked if she has a favorite, Madame Alexander replied, "Does a mother have a favorite child? I love them all."

7½″ Straight leg non-walker dressed in #365-1953. Has her original "Wendy Ann" booklet. Tag: Alexander-kin. The dress is dark blue with white polka dots with attached organdy pinafore/apron. (Courtesy Linda Crowsey)

7½″ "Wendy Ann" 1953. Straight-leg non-walker and very heavy in weight. Shown in original case that is same color pink inside as the Alexander boxes. The case is cloth covered with many flowers imprinted and interior is pink. Marks: Alexander-kin/Madame Alexander N.Y., on bottom of case. Has metal Fashion Award medal.

7½″ "Quiz-kin". 1953. (Wendy Ann). Non-walker with straight legs. Two buttons in back make head move. One-piece jersey panties, low cut round front and low V in back, organdy slip with loop braid trim. Same loop braid is used around sleeves and neck with lace around bottom (slip). Same loop braid and lace used on dress. Right side of dress crosses over in back and is tied with ribbon. No snaps on dress. Lace bonnet not original. Tag: Alexander-kins. (Courtesy Marge Meisinger)

7½″ "Little Edwardian" #415-1953, 1954 and 1955. Tag: Alexander-kins. Dress is blue with white polka dots. Bonnet has black net with flowers on top. Can be on a straight-leg non-walker or a straight-leg walker doll. (Courtesy Paula Ryscik)

7½″ Alexander-kins/Wendy Ann straight leg non-walker of 1953. All original and was an exclusive for FAO Schwartz in 1953. Pink check with inset organdy yoke and sleeves with rick rack trim. (Courtesy Loramay Wilson)

This FAO Schwarz catalog item sold for $12.95 in 1953. "Wendy Trousseau" is advertised as Madame Alexander's new minature doll. 7½″ in case with 19 pieces of varied clothes. Wears a pink and white jumper dress with lace trimmed organdy yoke and sleeves. Contents included a nightie, robe, taffeta dress, matching panties, flannel coat, bonnet, straw hat, pair of dress slippers, pair of socks, beach shorts, beach coat, beach bag, slip, panties, lace bonnet, roller skates, purse, curlers and comb.

8″ Wendy-kins in nylon party dress printed with clover blossoms. Tag: Alexander-kins. Was used in the 1955 trousseau set for Marshall Field, and also used by Marshall Field for St. Patrick's day with a green shamrock tied with green ribbons (at wrist). (Courtesy Dave and Kathy Ethington)

This "Wendy-Ann Trousseau" contained 19 pieces, and there was no full description of the suitcase in this FAO Schwarz 1955 catalog. (Sold for $12.95). Wendy Ann wears a flowered lace trimmed organdy dress, strap slippers and white socks. Included: a nightie and robe, white pique dress with matching panties, blue checked coat with hat, dress slippers, sunsuit, straw hat, curlers, comb, hangers, purse and roller skates.

8″ "Wendy-Ann". 1954 all hard plastic straight-leg walker. Blonde wig, blue sleep eyes. Original pink cotton night gown with lace trim and flowers at waist. Tag: Alexander-kins/Mme Alexander, etc. Alex., on back. (Courtesy Rita DiMare)

#442-1954 and tagged Alexander-kin. 8″ wears yellow dress and panties with black stripe pinafore and open top straw hat. (Courtesy Linda Crowsey)

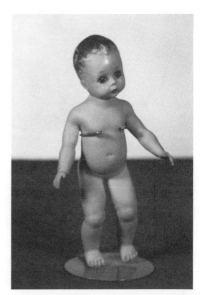

7½″ Molded hair Wendy-Kin baby to show the body style that is one-piece, stuffed vinyl. 1954.

Straight-leg walker dressed in ballerina outfit that is blue. Sold in 1954. Tag: Alexander-kin. (Courtesy Linda Crowsey)

8″ Straight-leg walker. 1955 matching pink tutu for the larger dolls. (#450). Two-piece. Tag: Alexander-kin, etc. (Courtesy Linda Crowsey)

8″ Straight-leg walker in two-piece red check pajamas. #425-1955. Tag: Alexander-kin. (Courtesy Linda Crowsey)

8″ "Best Man" #461-1955. Red wig, straight-leg walker. White dinner jacket and black trousers, maroon tie and cumberbund. Tag: Alexander-kin. (Courtesy Dave and Kathy Ethington)

8″ Groom Quiz-kin. Black felt jacket, gray trousers, silver tie, gray velvet vest. Straight leg, non-walker. Molded hair. Tagged: Alexander-kins. (Courtesy Dave and Kathy Ethington)

8″ Alexander-kin/Wendy in "Beach Outfit" #407-1955. Terry cloth with apple applique and matching headscarf. (Courtesy Sandra Crane)

8″ Alexander-kin #468-1955. Outfit for a train journey. Hat and coat are felt with metal buttons. Hat has lost shape. Coat has pleat in back. Shows the variation of print of the plaid used for skirt. (Courtesy Beth Donar)

8″ Straight-leg walker. #435-1955. Tag: Alexander-kin. White with red/blue trim. (Courtesy Linda Crowsey)

Dress top, under the coat of #468-1955. (Courtesy Beth Donar)

"Wendy" #440-1955. In garden dress of check with matching bonnet and plain pinafore. Came in various colors and checks. Catalog reprint.

This straight-leg walker is wearing #419-1955 and it was also sold boxed separately the same year. Tag: Alexander-kin. The hat and shoes are replaced. The dress came in various colors, this one is pink. (Courtesy Linda Crowsey).

8″ Straight-leg walker in "Maypole" #438-1955. Tag: Alexander-kin. Blue taffeta with organdy yoke and lace trim. The edge of lace around hem is attached to inside of dress. (Courtesy Linda Crowsey)

8″ Straight-leg walker dressed in pink with white eyelet pinafore, slip and panties. Tag: Alexander-kin, etc. #479-1955. (Courtesy Linda Crowsey)

8″ Alexander-kin dressed in #488-1955 and called "Garden Party." All original in organdy with lace trim and blue ribbons. (Courtesy Mariann's Doll House) (Billie McCabe)

8″ "Bride" #475-1955. Straight-leg non-walker. Juliet cap of lace and nylon tulle bridal veil. Gown of satin with tulle overskirt. Tag: Alexander-kin. (Courtesy Dave and Kathy Ethington)

#470-1955 "Gretel" in pink taffeta dress, printed cotton pinafore and bonnet. Catalog reprint.

#462-1955 "Wendy". Baby blue jacket of wool felt over a white polished cotton dress with pleated skirt. Blue bonnet. Catalog reprint.

8″ #483-1955 "Goes to Rodeo". White suede cloth trimmed with fringe and felt applique. Big sombrero hat and fancy boots. Catalog reprint.

#480-1955 "Baby Angel". White nylon tulle gown with white satin bodice, pink wings and silver halo and harp, flower trimmed. #488 "Garden Party" lace trimmed organza with pink picture hat. Catalog reprint.

1955-#472 "Curly Locks" in pale yellow taffeta and flowered pinafore, green bodice and lace cap. #489 "Bo-Peep" is in mauve taffeta with big panniers of rosebud print. Catalog reprint.

"Scarlett O'Hara". #485-1955. Flower print muslin with puff sleeves of tulle and big picture hat. Catalog reprint.

#487-1955 "Lady in Waiting to the Queen" dressed in pink satin with side ornaments of tulle and flowers. Coronet and veil. A really **rare** doll. Catalog reprint.

This is a catalog reprint of both 1956 "Southern Belle" dolls. (Southern Belle-Alexander-kin).

8″ Alexander-kin in #439-1955 (reverse side of rain set). Dress shown in next photo. Bend-knee walker. (Courtesy Beth Donar)

Dress under rain set #439-1955. Panties match the striped lining of coat and bonnet. (Courtesy Beth Donar)

8″ Bend-knee walker in blue taffeta with lace hat. Tag: Alexander-kin. #596-1956 and boxed extra. (Courtesy Linda Crowsey)

8″ #533-1956 and sold extra. Straight-leg walker. Dress is pink figured on white polished cotton. (Courtesy Linda Crowsey).

8" Alexander-kin dressed in #542-1956, but has the hat that belongs to the #591-1956 outfit. (Courtesy Dave and Kathy Ethington)

8" "Flowergirl". Bend-knee walker dressed in #543-1956. Tag: Wendy-kin. Matching dress to Little Genius #756-1956. White organdy. (Courtesy Linda Crowsey)

8" Alexander-kin in outfit #519-1956. Cotton dress that buttons down the back is grey and yellow. (Courtesy Jay Minter)

8" "Billie" shown in riding habit #571-1956. The pants are dark brown with beige insets and the shirt is white. The matching saftey hat is dark brown, as is the belt. Tag: Alexander-kins by Madame Alexander, etc. (Courtesy Ruth Fisher, England)

8" Alexander-kins #607-1956. Straight-leg non-walker. Rose bud print on Swiss organdy. (Courtesy Carole Nori).

8" Straight-leg walker in outfit that was sold extra #559-1956. Tag: Alexander-kin. Used a variation of trim, as braid was also used. (Courtesy Linda Crowsey)

8″ #556-1956. "Skater" with original bodysuit, but exact copy of original felt skirt. (Courtesy Linda Crowsey)

8″ Bend-knee walker. This was one of the dresses sold extra #517-1956. Tag: Alexander-kin. (Courtesy Linda Crowsey)

8″ Tagged: Alexander-kin blue dot suit. #026-1956. (Courtesy Linda Crowsey)

7½″ 1953 non-walker dressed in #518-1956. She has her original shoes, which are unusual side snap black patent. Tag: Alexander-kins. Was boxed as extra outfit with variation of prints or stripes used for this basic dress. (Courtesy Linda Crowsey)

8″ #595-1956. Blue gaberdine coat with white felt bonnet with blue ties and white/pink flowers. Bend-knee walker Alexander-kins. Originally had straw hat and purse. (Courtesy Margaret Mandel)

8″ "Wendy". Shows the dress under the blue coat #595-1956. Polished cotton with "roll" collar. (Courtesy Margaret Mandel)

8″ #605-1956 called "June Wedding". This gown came in pastel shades of peach, pale yellow, pale blue and pale green. (Courtesy Sandra Crane)

8″ #553-1956. "Off To School", with purse for milk money. Red striped cotton dress with plain top. (Courtesy Loramay Wilson)

8″ #586-1956. "Off On Shopping Spree". Blue check with white organdy pinafore apron. (Courtesy Loramay Wilson)

8″ "Wendy" in outfit #597-1956. Dotted swiss with lace trim. (Courtesy Jay Minter)

8″ Alexander-kin #592-1956. Pale green taffeta check sleeveless dress with matching bonnet. Replaced socks. Hair is straight and dark brown. This is the childhood doll of Pam Spirek and the wig has never been changed. (Courtesy Pat Spirek)

8″ "Wendy" in white sleeveless cotton dress with pleated skirt, blue striped knit sweater (on backward-catalog shows it buttoned down back and called "Basque Outfit"). Matching socks. Sailor hat. #574-1956. (Courtesy Pat Spirek)

8″ Left: #622-1956 "Rose Fairy." Jeweled gown of pink tulle, green velvet bodice piece, rose wand and large rose in hair to form crown. Right: #630-1956 "Cousin Karen" in flowered cotton with velvet bodice. Catalog reprint.

Groom with striped trousers was used from 1956 (#577) to 1963 (#421). This bride was used from 1966 (#735), #730 in 1968, through 1972. This one has a single row of lace around the skirt and the brides used from 1973 through 1978 have two rows of lace. (Courtesy Mary Williams)

"Wendy Ballerina Trousseau". The tutu is rose color. Also a gaberdine coat with velvet collar and matching poke hat, a taffeta afternoon dress with panties, organdy party dress with panties and slip, and silk pajamas and lace trimmed robe, plus shoes, socks and purse. In window type cardboard box. Cost in 1956 was $13.95. FAO Schwarz catalog.

8″ Bend-knee walker in an extra packaged dress #381-1957. Tag: Alexander-kins. This one is pink, but they came in various colors. Also sold in case (Ballerina) 1956. Replaced shoes. (Courtesy Linda Crowsey)

8″ Wendy as "Bridesmaid" #621-1956 with a different hat than shown in the catalog, although it is original to the doll. (Courtesy Bernice Heister)

"Wendy's Travel Trunk" was an exclusive for FAO Schwarz in 1956. 9″ square and over 4″ deep, this trunk is plastic covered, has a handle and four compartments for small items on one side, concealed behind a moveable panel. Doll fits on one side and can be seen through a clear plastic window. On other side is the wardrobe, five outfits, hangers. Trunk has decorated front and metal fasteners and came in red and blue. Trunk & doll sold for $19.75 in 1956.

This extra outfit for 1956 (#514) had an organdy pinafore. Dress in pink taffeta with blue ribbon. Tag: Alexander-kin. Also part of trunk wardrobe. (Courtesy Linda Crowsey)

"Wendy" in a red patent wardrobe case. Inside case is pink. All original and exclusive for FAO Schwarz. 1956. (Courtesy Marge Meisinger)

8″ Alexander-kin #591-1956. Had small oriental style hat. Coat came in various colors. This one is lined in blue. (Courtesy Beth Donar)

8″ "Wendy" #540-1956. Bend-knee walker. Taffeta red checked dress with bias white collar trim and matching panties. Tag: Alexander-kins. (Courtesy Dave and Kathy Ethington.

8″ Bend-knee walker in dress #379-1957. Yellow taffeta with pink appliques on skirt. Tag: Alexander-kin. (Courtesy Linda Crowsey)

8″ Wearing the pants and hat to #371-1957. The carcoat is missing. (Courtesy Linda Crowsey)

8″ "Wendy" #386-1957. Straight-leg non-walker. Sheer organdy dress with ruffles of val lace with straw hat. Tag: Alexander-kins. (Courtesy Dave and Kathy Ethington)

8″ Alexander-kin in #395-1957. Cotton dress and pinafore. Straw hat with flowers. (Courtesy Jay Minter)

8″ "Prince Charles" and "Princess Anne". #397 and 396. 1957. Bend-knee walkers. Navy blue suit on Charles and white lace dress with pink trim and pink trim hat on Anne. (Courtesy Sherry Kraft)

8″ Called "Tennis" #316-1957. Red and white striped shirt, red cotton shorts, tennis racket and glasses. Bend-knee walker. Tag: Alexander-kins. (Courtesy Bernice Heister)

8″ "Wendy" with bend-knees and a walker. Outfit is #586-1956 and also the dress with a short veil (flowers on head-piece) is the #395-1957 "First Communion" dress. White lace trimmed organdy with lace (rows) inset in front. Tag: Alexander-kins. (Courtesy Rita DiMare)

Wedding Party of 1957. "Wendy Bride" is in nylon tulle, "Bridesmaid" in pink nylon with hat, "Flowergirl" in blue dotted swiss and Watteau bonnet, "Bridegroom" in morning clothes and the "Little Minister" dressed in clerical garb, with glasses. This minister is one of the most desirable and rarest of the Alexander dolls. Catalog reprint.

8″ Bend-knees walker #400B (on box) 1959. Basic doll came in panties only. Dress purchased separately. Doll has brown hair and green eyes. Tag: Wendy-kins. 8″ "Little Genius" #215 (on box) 1959. Hard plastic head, vinyl body and limbs. Original with spoon and plastic bottle. Little knit booties with flowers, white cotton one-piece romper covered by pinafore. (Courtesy Bessie Carson)

8″ #583-1958 "Bridesmaid" in organdy embroidered with tiny flowers, pink sash and picture hat, bouquet of rosebuds. Catalog reprint.

8″ "Wendy" in long party gown of nylon and lace trim. Lace bonnet. Came in yellow, blue and green. 1958. #584. Catalog reprint.

8″ #532-1958 cotton dress with rick rack trim and shows the variations of prints used. Hat has been replaced.

8″ "Wendy" in #536-1958. Pale blue and white cotton with matching panties. White hat with red trim. Bend-knee walker. Tag: Alexander-kins. (Courtesy Bernice Heister)

8″ #532-1958 cotton dress with rick-rack trim. Hat is a replaced one. (Courtesy Jay Minter)

8″ Alexander-kin is an extra packaged outfit of 1958. This one is blue/white checked with a rose applique on skirt and white lace trim. It also came in red/white and yellow/white check. (Courtesy Linda Crowsey)

"Wendy's" 1958 circus dress is a plain cotton with a striped pinafore. White straw hat. The dress came in various colors. #561. Catalog reprint.

This red and pink organdy dress with white lace trim was sold packaged extra for the 8″ Alexander-kins in 1958. (Courtesy Linda Crowsey)

8″ "Wendy" #573-1958 with bend knees. Hat goes with another outfit and shoes are replaced. Dress is cotton, blue check with rows of lace trim. Tag: Wendy-kins. (Courtesy Sharon Ivy)

"Wendy" #542-1958. Cotton dress with braid trim and straw bonnet with ribbon bow. Catalog reprint.

"Wendy" in a 1958 (#569) dress of polished cotton trimmed with lace, velvet ribbon and tiny buttons on the bodice. Straw hat with streamers. Catalog reprint.

8″ "Wendy" in sheer dotted nylon party dress with lace trim, straw hat with flowers. 1958. #566. Catalog reprint.

"Wendy" had her hair in pig tails with this dress that is striped cotton with white collar and a plain pinafore. Hat is straw with ribbon trim. Came in several colors. 1958. #570. Catalog reprint.

8″ Alexander-kins #565-1958. Bend-knee walker. Tag: Wendy-kins. Pale pink dress with pinafore that is lace edged with two rows of trim. Lace around dress collar and cuffs. (Courtesy Sandra Crane)

8″ Alexander-kin bathrobe sold in extra package in 1958. Navy blue with red/white trim. (Courtesy Linda Crowsey)

1961 "Wendy" in suitcase as sold from the Marshall Fields catalog. Pink lace trim dress and carries a doll. Also sunsuit with pinafore, check dress, panties, straw hat and pajamas. Cost was $13.95.

8″ Alexander-kin dressed in #354-1962. This dress buttons down the back and has the Wendy Ann tag. Blue with white light flocked pattern and trim. (Courtesy Jay Minter)

8″ Alexander-kins "Ballerina" #420-1961 in gold-yellow. Bend-knee walker with blonde wig. (Courtesy Beth Donar)

8″ "Wendy" in #355-1962. Blue and white polka dot with red rick-rack and matching panties. Bend-knee walker. Tag: Alexander-kins. (Courtesy Bernice Heister)

8″ from about 1965-1966. Doll was purchased at a "Doll Hospital" that sold nude dolls. Bend-knee non-walker. The dress is from about 1961-1962. Tag: Wendy-kins. (Courtesy Susan Rogers)

8″ "Nurse with baby" #394-1963. Blue striped dress, white apron. Bend-knee walker. Tag: Alexander-kins. Blue/white striped dress. (Courtesy Beth Donar)

8″ Wendy-kin basic 600 doll of 1966 with original price tag of $1.98 (on box) dressed in riding habit that was purchased separately. Embroidered tag: Madame Alexander/New York/All Rights Reserved. Hair pulled to sides in ringlet curls. The "Ballerina" is #454 (on box) - 1955. Straight-leg walker. Separate panties with cotton net around legs, plastic head piece with two plastic flowers and woven threading, felt and buckrum flower at waist. Tag: Alexander-kins. (Courtesy Bessie Carson)

8″ "Bride" #470-1963 and matches the "Elise" #755-1963 and "Cissette" #755-1963. Tag: Wendy-kin, in back seam. (Courtesy Beth Donar)

8″ "Scarlett O'Hara". #785-1965. White satin-taffeta gown with green rick-rack, sash, ribbons and trim on sleeves. Pink cluster flowers. Natural straw hat. Green eyes. (Courtesy Susan Rogers)

8″ Wendy-kin #600-1966. Came in panties only. Dress purchased separately. Bend-knee walker. Dress is pink A-line cotton with three rows of lace on sleeves and two rows around neck. Embroidered flower stem and leaf with applied flower. Cotton separate slip with lace. Two metal snap closures. Tag: Wendy-kins. (Courtesy Bessie Carson)

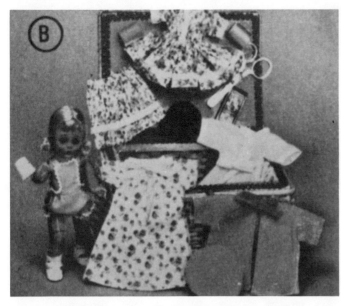

The 1969 "Sewing Basket" with the 8″ Alexander-kin was the same as in 1968, 1967 and 1966. This exclusive for FAO Schwarz has four complete outfits that are cut and ready to sew. The wicker case is 5½″ x 6½″ x 9″ and has a handle.

18″ and 14″ "Alice In Wonderland". All original. The 18″ is all hard plastic and dates from 1947. (Margaret). The 14″ is all composition and dates from 1937. (Wendy Ann). The statue also dates from the 1930's. (Courtesy Glorya Woods)

17″ (Sitting) "Alice In Wonderland" that is hard plastic and uses the "Maggie" mold. 14″ "Mary Ann" as Alice that began in 1966 and is still available. The small Alice is the 8″ Alexander-kin and dressed for Disneyland and Disney World from 1972, discontinued in 1976. The 17″ was made in 1950. (Courtesy Mary Williams)

This "Alice in Wonderland Trousseau" sold for $21.95 in 1951. Doll is 14″ and in a cotton print dress with organdy apron. The 14″, 18″ and 23″ Alice in Wonderland was also sold in 1951 in pale blue taffeta. (All: Maggie). FAO Schwarz catalog.

20″ "American Tot". All original with red mohair wig. Pressed cloth face (doll is all cloth), blue taffeta dress and bonnet. 1935-1937. Tag: Madame Alexander/New York. (Courtesy Glorya Woods)

15″ Kate Smith's "Annabelle Trousseau" sold at FAO Schwarz in 1952. Dressed as little girl in Kate Smith's well loved book "Stories of Annabelle". Dressed in white dress with rick-rack trim and sweater. Trousseau includes bra, panties, girdle and bra set, two hangers, denim pedal pushers with sweater, saddle shoes, rayon petticoat, terry cloth robe, taffeta pleated skirt, nightgown, pique shirtwaist, socks, felt slippers, felt sandals and embossed robe, curlers, brush and comb. This outfit sold for $20.00 while another is listed but not illustrated-"a less complete wardrobe and doll is in an organdy dress" for $15.00. (Maggie).

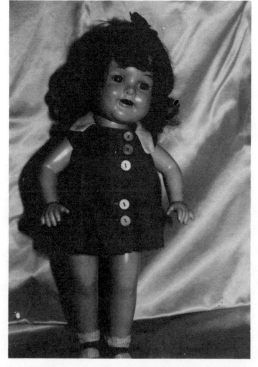

This is a movie wardrobe still showing "Aunt Pitty Pat" in the gown she wore to Melanie's picnic party in the movie "Gone With The Wind".

16″ "Baby Jane" (Juanita Quigley). All composition with brown sleep eyes, open smiling mouth and chubby cheeks. All original. (Courtesy Marge Meisinger)

Shows "Baby Jane" (who is Juanita Quigley) holding two dolls that are more than likely "Baby Jane" dolls by Madame Alexander and date from 1935 and 1936. Both head and clothes would be tagged. (Photo courtesy Marge Meisinger)

14″ "Baby Ellen". #3715-1965. 1972 was last year made. All vinyl using the Sweet Tears mold. Marks: Alexander/1965, on head. (Courtesy Renie Culp)

22″ "Baby Genius" of 1942. All original. Cloth body with composition head and limbs. Sleep blue eyes and glued on mohair wig. (Courtesy Mary Williams)

20" "Baby Lynn". #7135-1975. Cloth and vinyl. Marks: Alexander/1973, on head. This doll was made from 1973 to 1976 and then discontinued. Blue with pink pinafore. (Courtesy Renie Culp)

21″ "Baby Precious". #9010-1975. Cloth body with vinyl head and limbs. Sleep eyes and rooted hair. Made one year in pink and white romper suit. Marks: Alexander/1973, on head. (Courtesy Renie Culp)

20″ "Baby Lynn". #7020-1973. Cloth and vinyl. Marks: Alexander/1973, on head. Blue with white pinafore. (Courtesy Renie Culp)

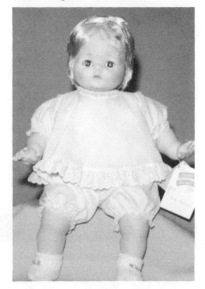

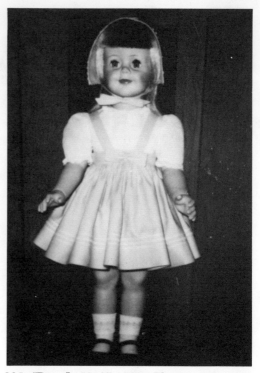

"Barbara Jane" came in one size only in 1952. (29"). Cloth body with stuffed vinyl head and limbs. She had various outfits, both organdy and cotton dresses. Catalog reprint.

30" "Betty" #3107-1960. Plastic and vinyl. Rooted hair. (Joanie). Original blue and white outfit, except shoes and socks are replaced. (Courtesy Doris Richardson)

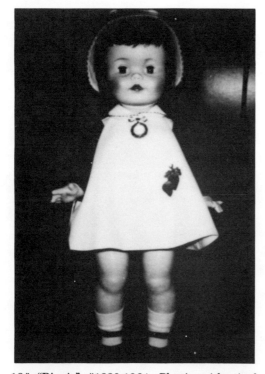

18" "Binnie" #1830-1964. Plastic with vinyl head and arms. Sleep eyes and rooted hair. Came with purse and watch at collar. (Courtesy Doris Richardson)

18" "Binnie". 1964. Came dressed in bright blue cotton trimmed with white braid and appliqued strawberries. Catalog reprint.

To identify between the all hard plastic walkers "Binnie" and "Winnie" is difficult. About the only difference is the hair styles. Winnie has a glued on feather cut wig, with small part on top and combed in all directions.

Binnie's hair is rooted to a vinyl skull cap, like the American Character Sweet Sue, and has longer part and bangs.

The later Binnies with bending knees and vinyl arms had glued on wigs.

"Binnie Walker" of 1954 and came in 15″, 18″ and 25″ sizes. Striped cotton dress with velvet bodice and braid trim on skirt. Hard plastic walker, head turns. Has flat feet. (Cissy). Catalog reprint.

18″ "Binnie Bride". All hard plastic. Walker with flat feet. 1950 (Binnie). Tagged: Madame Alexander, etc. (Courtesy Renie Culp)

1954 15″ "Binnie" in suitcase as sold from Marshall Field catalog. She is dressed in organdy with a net trimmed half slip/panties, short socks and black slippers. Rayon gaberdine coat, matching pillbox hat, white gloves and muff of fake leopard, tartan school dress, nightgown, playsuit, blouse, pedal pushers, bonnet and extra shoes, socks and curlers. Walker, head turns. Case: 17 3/8″ x 12 x 5. Sold for $19.95 in 1954.

15″, 18″ and 25″ "Binnie Walker" 1955. Wears a pinafore of striped pique over a ruffled, polished cotton dress, trimmed with braid and tiny pearl buttons. Hoop petticoat has ruffles of nylon net. Straw hat. Catalog reprint.

15″, 18″ and 25″ "Binnie Walker". 1955 with jointed knees and elbows came in this dress that is taffeta in tiny checks and trimmed with four rows of rick-rack, hoop petticoat, straw hat and has rhinestone on bodice. Catalog reprint.

15″ "Binnie Walker Skater". #1517-1955. Also came in 18″ size. Bright pink skirt and matching bonnet of wool felt, black jersey leotard trimmed with felt flowers and gold braid. (Courtesy Sandra Crane)

14″ "Binnie Walker". All original, except shoes. Red/white cotton dress, straw hat with red/white flowers. Flat-footed walker. All hard plastic. #1512-1955. (Courtesy Elizabeth Henderson)

17″ "Binnie Walker". #1824-1955. All original in red taffeta dress trimmed in white rick-rack. Navy and white checkered coat, lined in red taffeta. Pique white eyelet collar. Has unusual skull cap with black rooted hair. Childhood doll of Sue Conners.

"Binnie Walker's Trunk Trousseau" of 1955 sold in the FAO Schwarz catalog for $25.00. It is not listed as being an "exclusive". The doll is 15″ tall and the trunk is 16″ tall, made of white enamel with brass corners and lined in pink. Doll is wearing a pink woven cotton dress with white jersey cardigan and hat to match. A pink hooped nylon petticoat keeps dress skirt full. Also, pink tricot nightie, pink ruffled nylon robe, a white dress trimmed with red rick-rack and panties, blue denim pedal pushers with red silk blouse and a navy blue coat with red nylon lining and straw hat. Slippers, shoes, comb and hair curlers were also included.

"Binnie Walker" in a white metal trunk in skater's outfit. The doll is 15″ tall. 1955. Catalog reprint.

BINNIE IN CASE—No. 218—15" DOLL

This 15″ "Binnie Walker" came in a red metal train case in 1955. Her dress is white taffeta with red dots. This is the dress under the redingote (shown in case) and the two pieces together are #1518-1955. Catalog reprint.

25″ "Binnie Walker" - 1955. All hard plastic, walker, head turns. (Cissy). Vinyl over-sleeved arms, jointed at elbows. Jointed knees. Long formal of pink satin. Overdress caught up with roses, hoop skirt, rosebuds in hair. Catalog reprint.

7″ "Blue Boy" . Although referred to in brochures and catalogs as "Little Blue Boy", there is no "Little" on the tag: Fiction Doll/Blue Boy/Madame Alexander/New York. All composition, painted eyes to side. (Tiny Betty)(Courtesy Jay Minter)

1954 introduced "Bonnie" in the 12″, 16″, 19″ and 30″ sizes. (Kathy with wig). All vinyl, sleep eyes and open/closed mouth. Dressed in cotton romper and felt sandals. Catalog reprint.

FAO Schwarz listed this "Bonnie Baby" in basket as "Our Own Creation" in 1955, and it cost $28.00. Pink trimmed wicker basket with hinged cover and carry handles, mounted on legs with a lower shelf. 13″ doll with rooted hair, dressed in pink Swiss organdy dress, shell pink taffeta slip and panty, socks and shoes. Also pink taffeta coat and bonnet, cotton playsuit with poke bonnet, sweater, wash cloth and towel set, soap, beads, hot water bag, powder puff and hangers.

19″ "Bonnie" #5665-1954. Cloth and vinyl with blonde rooted hair with topknot, open/closed mouth and blue sleep eyes. White organdy dress with lace trim and tucks on bodice. Pink satin sash gathered at three places in front. Lace trimmed pink taffeta underslip and panties. White kid tie shoes with metal tipped laces. Tag: Madame Alexander. Marks: Alexander on head. (Courtesy Kathleen Rudisill)

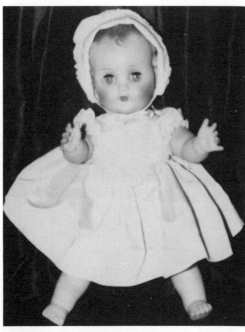

12" "Bonnie". 1955. One-piece stuffed vinyl body. Molded hair and sleep eyes. Clothes tagged. (Courtesy Mary Williams)

16" and 19" "Bonnie of 1955 came in this redingote of linen type fabric (various colors) with matching bonnet, worn over a dress of organdy, lace trimmed. #6735-1955. (Courtesy Doris Richardson)

BRENDA STARR by DALE MESSICK

Brenda Starr, star newspaper reporter, was born to be an eternal young woman in her twenties. She began as an adventuress in a small two-page comic book suppliment in the comic section. This was in June 1940, and on April 13, 1941 Brenda Starr entered the full sized tabloid. The strip "Brenda Starr" began exclusively in *The Chicago Tribune*, but by 1946 was syndicated throughout the U.S.

Dalia Messick, creator of Brenda Starr, took the name Dale for the strip. She was born in Gary, Indiana, studied art and began illustrating greeting cards. Liking fashions, Brenda Starr emerged as most fashionable, with none to match her seemingly endless string of beautiful clothes. Dale Messick says that Brenda is modeled after Rita Hayworth, but named after debutante Brenda Frazier, so much in the news during the years Brenda was "born".

By 1941, Brenda Starr had become the gorgeous and glamorous woman that she remains today. Brenda had numerous "almost" trips to the altar and a great many male admirers, but always there was Basil St. John, who had a gentic malady that caused him to black out periodically and forget that he was trying to find a cure. After adventures and mis-adventures over the years, Basil St. John developed a black orchid serum that controlled his illness and in January 1976 finally married the ever-young Brenda Starr. Her wedding gown was white velvet edged in mink and flowing with chiffon. The empire bodice was covered with stars and the tulle, tiered veil was crowned with a headpiece of jeweled stars. In September of 1977 their baby was born, and named Star-Twinkle. For Brenda Starr buffs, the 1978 Spegiel catalog carried the Playpal (marked 1975) Star-Twinkle doll.

Dale Messick is 71 years old, and one of the very few successful female comic strip designers in the world. When asked, she says she has had fun.

11½" "Brenda Starr" #920-1964. All original and in original box. (Courtesy Bessie Carson)

"Brenda Starr" in the pink gown #1020-1964 and shows the original hair-piece that came boxed with the doll. (Courtesy Roberta Jackson)

"Brenda Starr Bride" #1030-1965. Mint and original. The Brenda Starr doll was also used as the Yolanda, which also came in bride outfit. (Courtesy Roberta Lago)

This is a typical drawing of Brenda Starr, and comes from the *Chicago Herald Tribune*. (Courtesy Marge Meisinger)

The beautiful Brenda Starr finally landed her dream man in this January 18, 1976 comic strip. (Courtesy Marge Meisinger)

12″ "Brenda Starr". #960-1964. Hard plastic with vinyl arms and head. Sleep blue eyes/molded lashes. Jointed, swivel knees. Rooted hair. Tag: Brenda Starr/by Madame Alexander/New York USA. (Courtesy Margaret Mandel)

17″ "Pink Bride". 1950. All hard plastic with blue eyes (Margaret). Pink satin gown and pale pink veil with lace trim. Pink flowers in hand and on veil. Still has original gold tag on wrist. (Courtesy Mary Williams)

This shows another "pink" bride using the Margaret face. It is identical to the other, so there should be no question that perhaps one outfit was dyed pink someplace along the line. (Courtesy Vita Pennington)

25″ "Bridesmaid". #2546-1955. Had circlet of flowers in hair. Nylon tulle over taffeta gown. Flat feet. All hard plastic with vinyl over-sleeved arms, jointed at elbows. Tag: Madame Alexander, etc. (Courtesy Barbara Schilde)

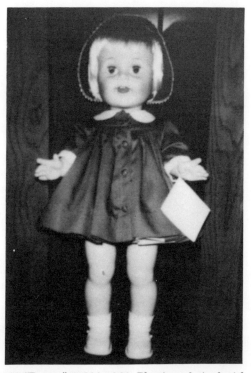

19″ "Pink Bridesmaid". Made of all rigid vinyl using the Margaret mold. The Wedding Party included "Bride" and the "Bridesmaids" in pink, pale blue and lavender. The gowns are organza with narrow silver braid at hem and silver slippers. Pink rosebuds in mohair wig and she carries rose bouquet with silver streamers. Box is marked: Style number 8400. 1952-53. (Courtesy Donna Colopy)

18″ "Bunny" #1820-1962. Plastic and vinyl with sleep eyes and rooted hair. Pique coat and bonnet. (Courtesy Doris Richardson)

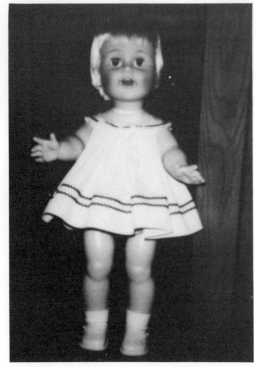

18″ "Bunny" shown in the dress (#1816) under the coat #1820-1962. White pique with red trim. (Courtesy Doris Richardson)

14″ "Butch". 1950-51. Cloth with early vinyl head and limbs. Blue sleep eyes, molded and painted hair. Came in three outifts including a white christening gown, white and blue two-piece slacks and shirt and a pink romper set. Marks: Alexander, on head. (Courtesy Mimi Hiscox)

Called "Perky Joan Trousseau" this Caroline was offered in the 1961 FAO Schwarz catalog for $29.95. Doll wears a blue nylon lace trimmed party dress with matching panties and slip. She also has pink silk-lined flannel coat and matching hat, rose pique play dress and matching shorts, a coolie hat and bag to match. Also included is a flowered nylon tricot pajama set and lace trimmed robe, bedroom slippers, mirror, comb and brush. The model's case is 14″ and of blue leatherette with a carrying handle.

12″ size of "Cherub" in 1960 with rosebud printed flannel wrapper and matching diaper. Came in this lace and taffeta covered cradle. Tiny taffeta pillow and lace trimmed taffeta coverlet lined with rosebud flannel. Catalog reprint.

12″ size of "Cherub" in 1960 with rosebud printed flannel wrapper and matching diaper. Came in this lace and taffeta covered cradle. Tiny taffeta pillow and lace trimmed taffeta coverlet lined with rosebud flannel. Catalog reprint.

12″ "Cherub". #3725-1961 in christening gown. All vinyl, but the 26″ size has a cloth body. (Courtesy Doris Richardson)

10″ "Cissette" in #942-1957. Pink organdy dress with satin ribbon tie and straw hat. Also came in white. Tag: Cissette. (Courtesy Linda Crowsey)

10″ "Cissette Matinee" #943-1957. Dress and jacket. Tag: Cissette. (Courtesy Linda Crowsey)

C

#944-1957. 10″ "Cissette" in pink polished cotton dress with wide lace collar. Hat has pink flowers. (Courtesy Loramay Wilson)

10″ "Cissette". The red/white dress is #0733-1962. The real mink fur is with outfit #0926-1957. (Courtesy Charmaine Shields)

This is the "Cissette Travel Trousseau" of 1957 that was an exclusive in the FAO Schwarz catalog. The case is plastic with a full "window" on one side.

10″ "Cissette" dressed in #945-1957. Blue with white polka-dots, polished cotton dress with wide val lace collar. Hat with flowers and wide pink ribbon tie. (Courtesy Loramay Wilson)

10″ Cissette as Bridesmaid #852-1958. The gown is tulle decorated with flowers and rhinestones, with soft cotton attached slip. Large picture hat with pink roses and green velvet bow and streamers in back. Cissy had matching outfit #2282-1958. (Courtesy Virginia Jones)

10″ "Cissette" in #876-1958. Bridal wreath design. Matches the #1750-1958 "Elise Bride". Floor length veil with flower design. Pearl necklace and earrings. Pink flower garter with rhinestone. Tag: Cissette. Marks: Mme. Alexander, on back. (Courtesy Kathleen Rudisill)

10″ "Cissette" in #830-1958. Jointed knees. (Courtesy Bessie Carson)

10″ Cissette dressed in #820-1958. Navy taffeta with lace around sleeves, pearl necklace and organdy stole, with large pink rose. Straw hat with tulle and pink rose. Cissy had matching outfit #2146-1957. (Courtesy Virginia Jones)

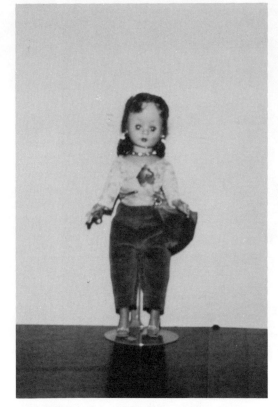

This "Cissette Travel Trousseau" was an exclusive with FAO Schwarz, and sold through their catalogs in 1958. The trunk is 12″ and made of fiberboard.

10″ "Cissette" in #807-1958. Velvet pants and lace blouse with sash that is starched chiffon. (Courtesy Loramay Wilson)

"Cissette Queen Travel Trousseau" sold in the 1959 FAO Schwarz catalog for $22.95. The case is 13″ X 12″ and is plastic with tubular metal frame, with zipper closing. Dressed in white brocade gown and blue sash. Also included was a lace robe, pink crepe nightie, pink polished cotton street dress with straw hat, petticoat, panties and mules.

10″ "Cissette Bride" #740-1959. Original. White nylon net over satin. Has "diamond" ring, silver shoes and wears garter. Tagged Cissette. (Courtesy Pat Spirek)

The 1960 FAO Schwarz catalog shows this "Cissette Bridal Trousseau" as an exclusive item. It sold for $21.75. Gown and veil are nylon tulle. 12″ metal wardrobe trunk. Also included are: flowered crepe robe, pink crepe nightie, a blue and white print street dress of polished cotton, straw hat, petticoat and panties and mules.

This is the basic #800-1960 Cissette in her navy blue sun-bathing suit. Tag: Cissette. (Courtesy Linda Crowsey)

10″ "Cissette" in three piece suit and hat. Tag: Cissette, etc. #810-1961. Sold boxed extra, also for the 10″ Jacqueline. (Courtesy Linda Crowsey)

Two Cissette dresses. One is pink and other is white. The white one has a single row of lace around the neck and the lace at hem is under the hem. The pink one has two rows of lace at the neck and the lace at the hem is on top. (Courtesy Virigina Jones)

Two Cissette undergarments. One is taffeta with gold trim and straps, and rhinestones. This one is lavender, but they came in several shades. The other is lace with pink elastic shoulder straps and pink ribbon trim with a rosette. Cissy also had this style, in black, pink, white and yellow. (Courtesy Virginia Jones)

11″ "Cissette". Body marked very faintly: Mme. Alexander. Dress tag: Cissette, as is wrist booklet. Black and white two piece suit of either challes or rayon. White collar and blouse. Rhinestone earrings and ring. (Courtesy Barbara Jean Male)(Photo by Michael Male)

20″ Cissy in #2097-1955 from the Portrait set a "Child's Dream Comes True". Blue satin gown has three sapphire color stones at neckline. White and silver braid trim forms design on front of gown. Flower coronet in hair and she carries an ostrich feather fan. (Courtesy Marian Schmuhl)

20″ "Cissy Bride" from "A Child's Dream Comes True" series. #2101-1955. Satin brocade gown with sprinkling of lace and seed pearls on skirt. Pearl earrings. Tag: Cissy by Madame Alexander. (Courtesy Charmaine Shields)

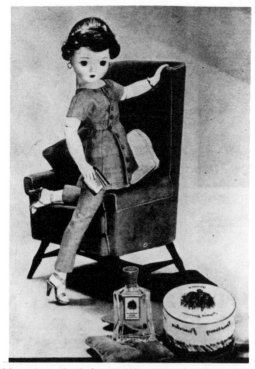

Magazine ad of the 1950's using the Cissy doll for Yardley of London. It is not known if the outfits the doll wore in the ads were ever placed on the market.

In 1956 you could purchase this "Cissy Takes a Trip" from the FAO Schwarz store for $55.00. The trunk is 24″ x 12″ x 11″ metal-covered wood. Included is a blue full-skirted, lace trimmed net gown over a lace trimmed taffeta underskirt and hooped organdy petticoat with a flower on each shoulder. Also a red print cotton full-skirted sundress with white rick-rack trim and large matching bow. Lace trimmed silk nightie and flowered nylon negligee. She is wearing a taffeta-lined black and white flared skirt over a red can-can petticoat, white pique blouse with Peter Pan collar and matching balero jacket. White straw hat, black high heel sandals and nylon stockings. Accessories are silver evening slippers, flowered mules, nylon stockings, handbag, gloves, sunglasses, comb, brush and mirror.

"Cissy" in extra outfit that was sold in 1956. #2016. Rows of pink roses, dark pink satin sash and straw purse and hat. (Courtesy Charmaine Shields)

20″ "Cissy" in red dotted Swiss organdy shirtwaist style dress of 1956. White can-can taffeta petticoat, straw hat with flowers and veil. #2019 - Catalog reprint.

"Cissy" #2012-1956. Mint and original in red satin dress with a drop waist, low neckline and white hat with red flowers. (Courtesy Charmaine Shields)

21″ "Cissy" #2039-1956. Long red satin gown with pleated waist sash in front. "Diamond" broach ties. Tag: Cissy by Madame Alexander. (Courtesy Charmaine Shields)

21″ "Cissy" #2040-1956. Mint and original. (Courtesy Charmaine Shields)

21″ "Cissy" shown in lavender satin afternoon gown with sash tie pulled to side. She has flowers at neckline and waist. Rhinestones set at neckline. Tag: Cissy by Madame Alexander. #2035-1956. (Courtesy Charmaine Shields)

The 1957 "Cissy Takes A Trip" was an exclusive with FAO Schwarz and sold for $55.00. The trunk is 24″ tall, and doll was dressed in a "Bon Voyage" outfit with full-flared skirt with striped cotton tailored blouse and chatelaine watch, coche hat, high heel shoes and nylon hose. Trunk items are: evening gown with underskirt and hooped petticoat, print cotton full-skirted sundress with rick-rack trim, slacks, white nylon lace trimmed blouse, lace trimmed silk nightie and flowered nylon negligee. Also, gold evening slippers, flowered mules, nylon stockings, flower trimmed fan, handbag, sunglasses, comb, brush and mirror.

21″ "Cissy" #2146-1957 dressed in navy satin afternoon dress with white stole and matching hat. The flowers are pink roses. She wears see-through gloves with a wrist ruffle. The pumps are navy and the earrings are pearls. Tag: Cissy by Madame Alexander, etc. 1956. (Courtesy Charmaine Shields)

"Cissy" is shown in an extra outfit sold in 1957 and box #2104. Called "Gardening", the jumper pants are orange and the front tie shirt top is blue. (Courtesy Charmaine Shields)

20″ "Cissy" #2113-1957. Polished cotton with gold print. (Courtesy Barbara McKeon)

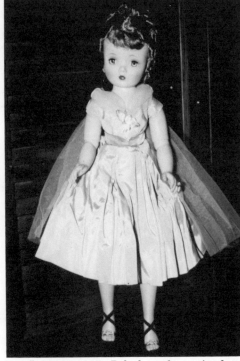

"Cissy" #2128-1957. Pale lavender satin dress has an attached drop stole of chiffon and velvet sash. (Courtesy Charmaine Shields)

"Cissy" #2130-1957. Blue polished cotton dress with lace trim and sleeve cuffs. Blue straw hat, pink flowers. (Courtesy Charmaine Shields)

20″ "Cissy" that is all hard plastic with vinyl over-sleeved arms, jointed at elbows and knees, is shown in an original half slip and bra. Ca. 1957. (Courtesy Renie Culp)

"Cissy" #2120-1957. This mint and original doll shows this dress to its best advantage. (Courtesy Charmaine Shields)

"Cissy" #2174-1957. This beautiful gown is deep purple and pale lavender with large corsage of flowers at edge of dropped hip line. (Courtesy Charmaine Shields)

21" "Cissy" #2143-1957 and 10½" "Cissette" #943-1957 in matching lavender with separate jackets. Rosette at neckline and on skirt. "Cissette" has straw (lavender) hat, carries matching purse and her shoes are lavender. "Cissy" is wearing lavender shoes with blue flower across toes. (Courtesy Charmaine Shields)

21" "Cissy" in #2283-1958 "Dolls To Remember" series. The gown is silk with pink camellias. The long cape stole is velvet and lined of same materials as gown. She has a gold net veil attached to flowers that can be worn over the face (unseen as in back of doll). (Courtesy Charmaine Shields)

21" "Cissy" in extra gown sold in 1958-#2254, "Dolls To Remember". Pale lavender satin with dotted swiss over it, and an attached matching dotted swiss stole. Pink rose corsage bouquet at waist. (Courtesy Charmaine Shields)

C

21″ "Cissy Bride" #2280-1958 of the "Dolls To Remember" series. There was a matching 16½″ "Elise Bride" in 1958-#1750. Gown is lace with embroidered bridal wreath pattern. Veil of tulle is attached to a coronet of flowers. Originally had pearl necklace and bracelet. Wears solitaire ring. (Courtesy Charmaine Shields)

21″ "Cissy" #2282-1958. All original in tulle ballgown with pink and white flocked flowers with rhinestones. Ruffled hat with flower trim. Elbow gloves, pierced ears and solitaire. (Courtesy Elizabeth Henderson)

21″ "Cissy" #2026-1958. Dressed in heavy brocade red satin evening gown. Has matching stole caught with large white flower. Red roses in hairdo. The slippers are red. Tag: Cissy by Madame Alexander, etc. Original price tag on doll is for $21.95. (1958). (Courtesy Charmaine Shields)

21″ "Cissy" dressed in #2228-1958, an extra outfit boxed and sold that year. Blue/white checked cotton with organdy sleeves/lace trim and a black belt. (Courtesy Charmaine Shields)

"Cissy" #2218-1958. Shirt blouse is white, with burnt orange polished cotton skirt. The jacket and tam is white rabbit fur. (Courtesy Charmaine Shields)

21" "Cissy" dressed in dotted black polished cotton with white trim. #2210-1958. The braid hat is white and the tie is dotted swiss. Red/white flowers and black purse that is plastic with red flower. The shoes are black with white ornament across toes. Tag: Cissy by Madame Alexander, etc. (Courtesy Charmaine Shields)

21" "Cissy" shown in outfit #2211-1958. Polished cotton dress with white buttons, sleeve edges. Came with either red or white straw hat with flowers and veil, which could be worn tied under the chin. (Courtesy Charmaine Shield)

21" "Cissy" in #2232-1958. Modified shirtwaist dress. Matches the "Elise" #1732 of this same year. These dresses (for both dolls) came in variations of print and color. (Courtesy Charmaine Shields)

Clothes for "Cissy" in the FAO Schwarz 1959 catalog. (C) Lace robe; (D) Pink crepe nighty; (E) Striped skirt and sweater; (F) Petticoat and panties; (G) Red evening gown; (H) Coral wool coat and hat/also came in royal blue.

20″ "Cissy". Has auburn hair and bisque-like hard plastic. Vinyl over-sleeved arms that are jointed at the elbows. Is shown in original pink nightgown with lace trim. Tagged Cissy. #22-20-1958. (Courtesy Sue Conner)

20″ Cissy in "Royal Tour Trousseau" a $75.00 (then), exclusive for FAO Schwarz in 1960. Her gown is gold brocade, and she is in a 24″ metal, covered trunk. She has a tea dress, print dress, cloak, sports slacks, silk nightie and robe, chemise, shoes, mules, stockings and accessories.

21″ Cissy Bride #2170-1959. (Courtesy Charmaine Shields)

Nude "Coco" with brown eyes and eyeshadow. Jointed at waist with lower torso and legs all molded in one piece. (Courtesy Margaret Mandel)

20″ "Coco" in full length black and white printed jersey jumpsuit, yellow satin ankle length coat. 1966. Catalog reprint.

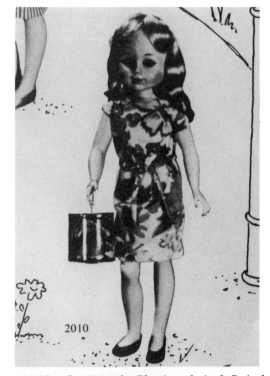

20″ "Coco". 1966 only. Plastic and vinyl. Swivel waist with legs molded in "model" positon. Printed silk knitted sheath.

20″ "Coco" in black skirt and short orange cotton waist-length jacket. 1966.

20" "Coco" shown in one of the dresses available for her in 1966. Pin-striped sheath dress edged with ruffled organdy at neck and sleeves.

37" "Clarabell" doll patterned after a character on the "Howdy Doody" show. (Bob Keeshan played the role at one time. He is now Captain Kangaroo). Cloth body and limbs and cloth mask face. Eyes are yellow daisies with brown pom pom centers. Belt around waist holds cardboard box-lettered: Clarabell by Madame Alexander. Wears paper label, daisy shaped: Posey Pets/by/Madame Alexander. On reverse side is: Flowery eyes on/our/Posey Pets/with nose of rose/or flower-ettes/when these features/on a toy you see/these are made by/Alexander Company. The flowered features for the face identify Alexander Posey Pets. Clarabell also came in 19", 29" and 49" sizes. 1951-1953. (Courtesy Nancy Arnott)

19" Clarabelle from the Howdy Doody T.V. Show of 1951. All stuffed heavy canvas with the head having three seam lines. Felt features with flower eyes/bead centers. Felt ears and yarn hair. Tag: "Clarabelle Clown"/Madame Alexander/New York, U.S.A. Gold paper wrist tag: Fashion Academy Award. (Courtesy Virginia Jones)

16½" "Country Cousin" using the Marybel doll. 1958. Dress is patch-quilt cotton and buttons down the back. Hair was originally set in braids.

Shows the tag on the 1958 "Country Cousin".

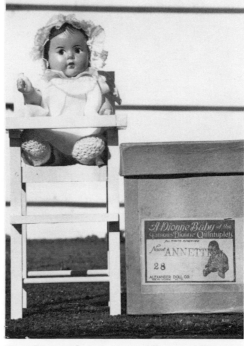

7½" Dionne Quint. 1936. All composition with molded brown hair and painted side glancing brown eyes. All original, including white wood high chair, which fits in original box with doll. "Annette" embroidered on bib. Marks: Dionne-Annette, on head. Alexander, on back. Tag: Dionne Quintuplets Annette-Exclusive License. Alexander Doll Co., N.Y. (Courtesy Clarice Kemper, photo by Clarice Kemper.)

14" Dionne Quint with a composition swivel shoulder head on a composition shoulder plate. Cloth body and composition limbs. 1936. Wig and sleep eyes. Marks: Dionne Madame Alexander. (Courtesy Barbara Schilde)

12" Twin "Dopey's" dressed in original clothes. Stiff bodies not made for sitting, composition shoulder plate. Doll not marked. Tag: Walt Disney's "Dopey" by Madame Alexander N.Y., N.Y. All Rights Reserved. (Courtesy Diane Hoffman)

9″ "Dutch". All composition. Doll is marked on body: Wendy Ann/Mme Alexander/New York. Tag: Dutch. (Courtesy Dianne Hoffman)

9½″ "Dutch Boy". All composition and original. Marks: Wendy Ann/Mme. Alexander/New York, on back. Tag: Madame/Alexander/New York U.S.A. Has side glancing painted eyes. 1935-1939. (Courtesy Pat Sebastian)

18″ "Edwardian" #2001A-1953. (Margaret). All hard plastic, flat-foot walker. Long pink hose, black center snap shoes. Floor length half slip of cotton with wide ruffle (hoop style), attached to short panties with lace trim on legs. "Fake" breasts of chamois. Black satin "poke" style bonnet with lace trim and rose feather. Black lace gloves. Pink on white embossed print gown. Tag: Madame Alexander/All Rights Reserved/New York U.S.A.

18″ "Elaine" from the "Me and My Shadow" series of 1954. #2035E and had matching 8″ Alexander-kin. Missing white straw lace picture hat. (Courtesy Sandra Crane)

16½" "Elise" is shown in #1632-1957. Chocolate brown jumper skirt and pink blouse. The hat is brown with pink flowers. (Courtesy Charmaine Shields)

16½" "Elise". #1636-1957 called "Junior League" (had white furry hat). Hard plastic and vinyl. Purple taffeta dress and white coat. Two-tone purple tie and purple heels. Heels are so high, the foot must be in the ballerina position to fit into the shoe. Can-can slip. Tag: Elise, on coat. Marks: Alexander, on head. Mme Alexander, on back. (Courtesy Kathleen Rudisill)

16½" "Elise". Hard plastic with vinyl oversleeved arms. Jointed knees, elbows and ankles. Pierced ears, sleep blue eyes, blonde wig. Blue sleeveless taffeta dress with matching balero jacket. Pink flowers at waist and in hair. Black strap pumps. Tag: Elise/Mme. Alexander. Alexander, on head. #1643-1957. (Courtesy Rita DiMare)

16½" "Elise" in #1732-1958. Modified shirtwaist dress in cotton print with lines and flowers. Purple straw hat with flowers. Doll has jointed ankles. Matches Cissy #2232-1958. (Courtesy Charmaine Shield)

16½″ "Elise" in extra outfit #16-40. Yellow striped bathing suit with white rick-rack trim and matching wrap skirt. Yellow straw hat with red and green ribbon (satin) and fruit. Also with this outfit were the low heeled shoes as pictured. Tag: Elise, on skirt only. Matching outfit for Cissette was #805. 1958. (Courtesy Kathleen Rudisill)

16½″ "Elise" jointed in three piece outfit of pink and white striped cotton. Blouse trimmed in white lace; coulotte under long pleated skirt. Long skirt only tagged Elise. Outfit bought separately from doll. (Courtesy Margaret Mandel)

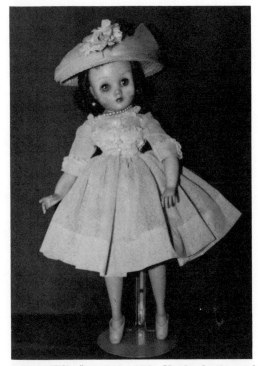

16½″ "Elise" #1718-1958. Hard plastic with vinyl oversleeve arms, jointed elbows and ankles. Flocked nylon dress. Marks: Alexander, on head. Tag: Elise by Madame Alexander, etc. All original except shoes. (Courtesy Florence Black Musich)

16½″ Elise outfit (sold extra) #16-45. The shorts are the ony ones that are tagged: Elise. Button down the front blouse and skirt. (Courtesy Virigina Jones)

"Elise" #1730-1958. Pale green chiffon over pale green satin sprinkled with pink roses. Mint and original. (Courtesy Charmaine Shields)

"Elise on Tour", an exclusive for FAO Schwarz in 1958. The trunk is 18″ tall. Clothes include blue formal, with under-skirt and hooped petticoat, silver high heel slippers, stockings and jewelry and bag. Also a dotted nylon dress with petticoat and panties and low heeled shoes. Pink crepe nightie, pink ballerina outfit of nylon tulle, satin bodice, trimmed with pink blossoms.

Clothes for "Elise" in the 1959 FAO Schwarz catalog: (D) Gold net ballet outfit; (E) Striped skirt and sweater; (F) Petticoat and panties; (G) Lace robe; (H) Pink crepe nightie; (J) Blue evening gown; (K) Coral wool coat and hat (also offered in royal blue).

16½″ "Elise" is shown in her original bride gown. #1835-1959. Pink chiffon over pink satin with lace on bodice and sleeves. Pink satin sash and flowers in her hair. Veil missing. (Courtesy Charmaine Shields)

E

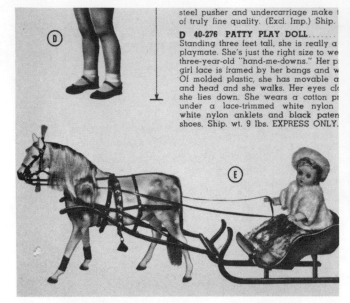

steel pusher and undercarriage make
of truly fine quality. (Excl. Imp.) Ship.

D 40-276 PATTY PLAY DOLL.........
Standing three feet tall, she is really a
playmate. She's just the right size to we
three-year-old "hand-me-downs." Her p
girl face is framed by her bangs and w
Of molded plastic, she has movable a
and head and she walks. Her eyes cl
she lies down. She wears a cotton pr
under a lace-trimmed white nylon
white nylon anklets and black paten
shoes. Ship. wt. 9 lbs. EXPRESS ONLY.

FAO Schwarz offered this "exclusive" in 1960. The horse is 15″ high and flocked. The 14″ sleigh is wood with red velvet upholstery and has a lined robe. The sleigh is painted red and green. 39″ overall. The Elise doll is 16″. During other years Schwarz offered this horse and sleigh rig with other dolls that were not Alexander.

"Elise" in #1730-1960. Blue satin with blue chiffon overskirt and attached chiffon stole with pink roses on skirt and shoulder. Used as an exclusive for FAO Schwarz in 1961. (Courtesy Charmaine Shields)

The FAO Schwarz catalog of 1960 shows this 16″ Elise in "Afternoon Dress". She sold for $15.00. Lace trimmed blue and white polka-dot cotton with wide sash and open puff sleeves. High heeled slippers and white straw hat with flowers.

An FAO Schwarz exclusive of 1961 was called "Lady Elise Trousseau". 16″ in an 18″ metal trunk. She wears a blue net gown trimmed with rosebuds over a double nylon taffeta crinoline. Other clothes include taffeta evening cloak, pink polished cotton street dress, taffeta slip and panties, a double skirted nylon nightgown and flowered taffeta robe. Also included is handbag, shoes, stockings, mirror, comb and brush. This trunk, clothes and doll sold for $42.95 in 1961.

"Elise" is dressed in an extra outfit sold in 1961, box #18-9. This is the bouffant hair Elise made for just one year. (Courtesy Deedie Shields)

16½″ "Elise" with the Kelly head. "Ballerina" #1740-1962. This Kelly head reduced to this size was only used one year. (Courtesy Renie Culp)

14″ #1750-1962. "Elise Bride". Listed in catalog as being 18″ tall. She has green sleep eyes. This bride also came with very dark wig. Hard plastic and vinyl. Note the very extended forefinger on the right hand. (Courtesy Renie Culp)

17″ "Elise" in orchid formal #1745-1963. Matches a Cissette and also #345-1963 Alexanderkin. Head is vinyl. (Courtesy Sandra Crane)

The 1964 "Elise On Vacation" was an FAO Schwarz exclusive and sold for $58.00. The doll is 16″ and came in a 20″ metal trunk. Doll is wearing blue lace trimmed evening gown of organdy, blue taffeta cocktail dress, red suit of gaberdine, riding habit with boots and hat, pink tulle ballerina outfit with slippers, extra undies, lace trimmed tricot nightgown, evening bag, masquerade mask, shoes, stockings and vanity set.

In the 1964 catalog FAO Schwarz called this Elise outfit "Elise at the Horse Show" and it sold for $12.95. Boots, jodhpurs, jacket and riding hat. Note hairdo, which is "pageboy".

17″ "Elise" #1740-1964. Has vinyl head. Skirt has five rows of lace. The matching Alexanderkin bride of 1964 as #679. (Courtesy Sandra Crane)

16½″ Elise with hard plastic body and vinyl head. #1720-1964. Satin and chiffon tu-tu is blue. The arms are vinyl over-sleeved and jointed at the elbows. She also has joints at the ankles. (Courtesy Charmaine Shields)

Called "Elise Takes A Trip", this 1966 item was an exclusive with FAO Schwarz. 17″ doll is packed in a 20″ metal trunk. Clothes included evening gown of pleated chiffon, cocktail dress with rows of lace and velvet bodice, checkered travel suit, tulle ballerina outfit with slippers, satin lounging pajamas, cotton dress with petticoat and lace trimmed silk nightie. This item cost $58.00 in 1966.

17″ "Elise Debutante" in chiffon gown with lace and sequin trim. "Queen Elise". Both were in the 1966 FAO Schwarz catalog.

1966 FAO Schwarz showed these Elise clothes in their catalog. (L.) Full skirted chiffon formal; (M.) Rose velvet bodice and full lace skirt cocktail dress; (N.) Black and white checkered suit; (P.) Bell-bottom lounging pajamas of turquoise satin; (R.) Red sheath dress; (S.) Pink crepe nightie.

17″ "Elise Bride" #1760-1966. The lace is "V-ed" on the bodice and there is lace around the veil. The later brides did not have the lace around the veil and they had two strips of lace from the waist to hem on front of gown. (Courtesy Mary Williams)

1967 clothes for 17″ "Elise" or "Maria" in the FAO Schwarz catalog. (K) Chiffon formal; (L) Blue cocktail dress; (M) Blue coat and beret; (N) White cotton dress with red trim; (P) Pink satin nightie; (R) Bell-bottom lounging pajamas.

The 1967 "Elise Takes a Tour" exclusive for FAO Schwarz has the same trunk as the 1966 one, but different clothes, although the handbag and brush/comb set is the same. Doll is 17″ tall and the metal trunk is 20″ tall. Cocktail dress is blue taffeta.

The 1968 FAO Schwarz catalog had these clothes listed for Elise. Included are an evening gown, nightie and robe, coat and two dresses.

FAO Schwarz offered this "Elise Takes a Trip" set for $58.95 in 1968. 17″ doll in a 20″ trunk. Clothes include gown with tiered lace skirt that she is wearing, cocktail dress of blue moire, a blue coat and beret, tulle ballerina outfit with slippers, pink cotton dress with panties, lace trimmed silk nightie, necklace, evening bag, handle bag, shoes, stockings and a vanity set.

1969 FAO Schwarz exclusive "Elise Takes a Trip" had a price increase to $65.00, and the quality of the clothes lessened. Still using the same metal trunk, this 17″ doll came in pink organza formal trimmed with lace, rose slacks, white organdy ruffled blouse, gold chain belt, blue cape and cap, plaid cotton dress, nylon lace trimmed pegnoir set, pink tulle ballerina outfit.

These clothes were sold from the FAO Schwarz catalog in 1970 for the Elise and Leslie 17″ dolls. Top to bottom: Maxi-coat and hat (coat in tiny check), slack set, street dress, robe, nightie, ballet outfit and evening gown.

17″ "Elise" in #1755-1970. Came in pink, yellow and blue. Most of these dolls were red-headed. Flowers in hair missing, otherwise she is original. The gown is just like the "Bride" this same year. (Courtesy Mary Williams)

1970 saw the continuation of the "Elise Takes a Trip" exclusive for Schwarz, now with a price of $68.50 and still using the same metal trunk, but now the trunk is 21″ tall. Included is a pink organza gown trimmed with lace, lounging outfit, street dress, nightie and matching robe and a maxi-coat.

These clothes were offered through FAO Schwarz in 1971, for the Elise doll (17″). Navy blue coat, red dress slack set, ballet, robe and nightie and pink lace trimmed gown.

The 1971 FAO Schwarz catalog carried this "Elise Take A Trip", and the cost was $75.00. The 21″ trunk is metal, and the clothes for the 17″ doll include pink organza, lace trimmed gown, lounging set, street dress, nightie and matching robe and a maxi coat. Also included was a pink tulle ballerina outfit.

This 1972 FAO Schwarz catalog shows "Elise" wearing the same gown that had been offered in 1971. The trousseau included lounging outfit, street dress, negligee and matching penoir, street coat, ballerina outfit and was in a metal trunk. The price of this outfit had increased to $75.00 in 1972.

17″ "Portrait Elise" #1780-1972. Plastic and vinyl with rooted hair. Discontinued 1974. (Courtesy Renie Culp)

17″ "Formal Elise". Was #1755-1973 and #1650-1975 and 1976. Discontinued in 1977.

16″ "Elise Bride" #1670-1975. Plastic and vinyl with rooted hair and sleep eyes. (Courtesy Diane Hoffman)

11″ "Fairy Princess". All composition with the Wendy Ann mold. Sleep eyes and mohair wig. All original. A cute and rare size. Marked Mme Alexander on head and tag. 1942. (Courtesy Marge Meisinger)

13″ Youngest member of the "Five Little Peppers". 1936. Shown in the Benson Distributor Catalog mid-summer 1936, but not in the 1937 one. Came in sizes 13″ and 16″. (16″ size not shown). All composition and has a fur wig. (Courtesy Joann Ide, photo by Dave Ide)

F

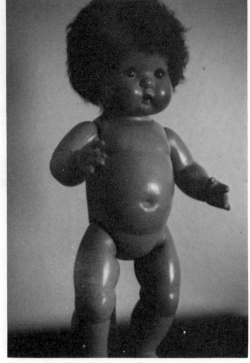

Shows the "Little Pepper" nude. Body marked Alexander. (Photo by Dave Ide)

The Benson Catalog of 1936 describes these original clothes as coming "in pastel shades of the rainbow". (Courtesy Joann Ide, photo by Dave Ide)

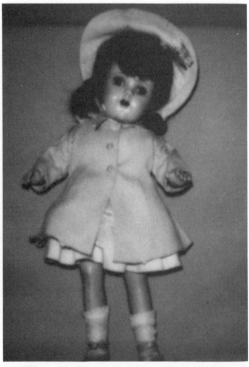

Set of the "Fisher Quints" with hard plastic heads on all vinyl bodies, sleep eyes and open mouth/nursers. In tagged "Quint" outfits that are "jumpsuit" type. 1964. (Courtesy Marge Meisinger)

14" "Flora McFlimsey". All composition, brown eyes and freckles. Pink gaberdine coat and matching bonnet. 1941-1942. (Courtesy Sharon Ivy)

16″ "Flora McFlimsey". All composition with freckles, sleep eyes and mohair wig. All original, dress, coat, muff and bonnet. Marked Princess Elizabeth/Alexander Doll Co., on head. High top, side snapped shoes. 1939. (Courtesy Glorya Woods)

Shows two different versions of the "Flora McFlimsey" doll. 15″ and 17″ all composition. Sleep eyes, open mouths and freckles. Same hair style, but different color clothes. Heads are marked Princess Elizabeth and tagged: Flora McFlimsey. 1939. (Courtesy Marge Meisinger)

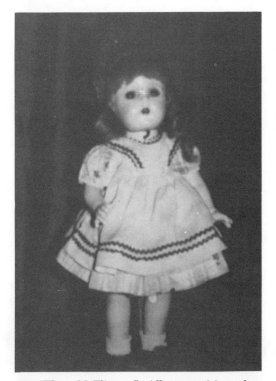

17″ "Flora McFlimsey". All composition, sleep eyes, open mouth and freckles. Red wig. Clothes are the original yellow with brown trim. Marks: Princess Elizabeth-Alexander Doll, on head. Flora McFlimsey of Madison Square by Madame Alexander N.Y., on tag. 1939. (Courtesy A.P. Miller Collection)

15″, 18″ and 25″ "Flowergirl" of 1954 (Cissy/Binnie). Nylon net and lace over taffeta, pink satin sash and circlet of flowers in hair. Flat-footed walker. Catalog reprint.

This is a newspaper account and photo of the "Freedom" and "Liberty" dolls (both Margaret and hard plastic), but the date cut and pasted to the photo is May 25, 1950 and all the other accounts of this event have been dated 1955. It has been reported that Dace Epermanis is a doctor. It is not known if she still has the dolls. (This scrapbook item courtesy Kathy Lyons.)

21″ 1968 "Gainsbourgh" #2184. Aqua and white gown. (Courtesy Barbara Schilde)

21″ Portrait "Gainsbourgh" of 1978. (Courtesy Renie Culp)

14″ "Gidget". Left: #1421-nautical dress and hat. Center: #1420 cotton formal. Right: #1415 pinchecked jumper. Registered as "The T.V. Girl" and called a typically "All American" teenager. 1966. Catalog reprint.

14″ Princess Elizabeth mold used for "Girl Scout". All composition with original mohair wig in pigtails. All original Girl Scout uniform of green chambray undies and matching dress. Kelly green socks and belt. Painted lashes under eyes only. Open mouth. Sold through the National Scout group. 1948-1949. (Courtesy Margaret Mandel)

18″ "Glamour Girl" of 1953-#2010A. All hard plastic and a walker. (Maggie). The gown is red taffeta with grey cape of fur-cloth. Brown sleep eyes. (Courtesy Pam Ortman)

13½″ "Godey Lady". (Margaret). All hard plastic. Apricot color gown. Cotton pantaloons with long white socks, attached cotton slip. Brown old-fashioned side snap shoes. Flower basket necklace with gold "thread" chain. 1949. Tag: Godey Lady/Madame Alexander, etc.

13½″ "Godey Lady Bride". All hard plastic (Margaret). Cotton, old-fashioned panties with blue ribbon ties. Princess style full length slip of cotton. Hose with satin front snap shoes. Satin gown with pannier drop front over princess style. Bustle back formed by elastic. Chin-tied ruffled lace cap veil. 1949.

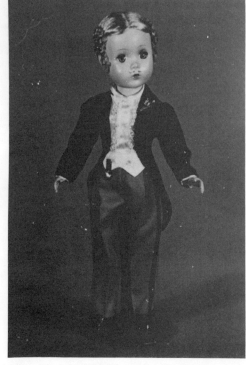

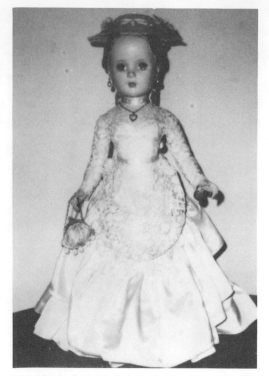

13½″ "Godey Man/Groom". All hard plastic (Maggie) with sideburns and over the ear curly hairdo. Tiny painted on mustache. One-piece pants and top, afternoon/groom coat, side snap black shoes. Tag: Madame Alexander, etc. Could be used with Godey Ladies or Godey Bride. 1949.

20″ "Godey" 1951. Hard plastic, flat feet. Doll not marked. Dress tag: Madame Alexander/All Rights Reserved/ New York U.S.A. Fashion Academy Award tag on wrist. Dress is cream taffeta with lace on bodice with matching purse and straw hat. Hat has lace, ribbon and flower trim. Pearl earrings (drop) and locket. Cream colored slip, silk stockings and cream colored slippers. (Margaret). (Courtesy Dave and Kathy Ethington)

1978 "Goldilocks" with the Mary Ann face. 14″ tall. (Courtesy Renie Culp)

8″ "Great Britain". The newest country to be added to the International line. 1978. (Courtesy Renie Culp)

7″ "Gretel". (Tiny Betty). All composition with painted eyes, shoes, socks. All original. 1937. Blue dress. (Courtesy Marge Meisinger)

14″ "Good Fairy". All hard plastic. (Margaret). Has small hands with all fingers slightly curled with thumb and little finger separate. Satin panties and half slip. Pink satin gown with flaired back, gold rick-rack trim and a blue button in front at neck. Yellow net/gold rick-rack wings. Replaced tiara. Pink satin slippers. Marks: Alex., on head. Tag: Good Fairy/Madame Alexander NY USA/All Rights Reserved. (Courtesy Margaret Mandel)

This is the tag on the "Good Fairy" doll owned by Margaret Mandel.

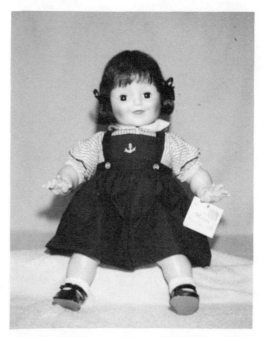

20″ "Happy" #5570-1970. Cloth with vinyl head and limbs. Rooted hair, wide open/closed laughing mouth and sleep brown eyes. Marks: Alexander/1970. Made one year only. (Courtesy Renie Culp)

14″ Heidi #1580-1976. This is the first year this doll was sold with a brown hat, prior dolls had natural color hats. (Courtesy Renie Culp)

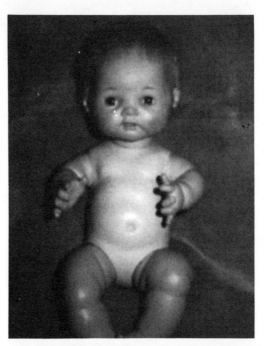

15″ "Honey Bea" or "Sugar Tears" of 1963. All vinyl with rooted hair and sleep eyes. (Courtesy Doris Richardson)

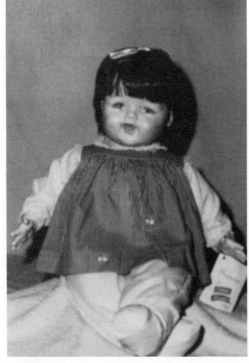

21″ "Big Huggums" #6840-1977 and 1978. Cloth and vinyl. Painted blue eyes, open/closed mouth with two molded lower teeth. All original. Marks: Alexander Doll Co. Inc., on head. (Courtesy Renie Culp)

ICE CAPADE DOLLS

Note: All dolls in this section are the courtesy of Marlowe Cooper and Patricia Smith.

When the owners of most of the large skating arenas got their heads together during 1940 and decided to produce their own show, their ambition was to create a skating carnival that would be entirely new and different.

They chose as their director Russell Markert, who from 1928 to 1933 produced shows at the Roxy Theatre in New York, organizing his famous Roxyettes, who later moved to Radio City Music Hall as the famous Rockettes. Between 1928 and 1940, he also staged the ensembles in "Animal Crackers", "Just A Minute", "Keep It Clean", "Here Goes The Bride", "Say When", George White's "Music Hall Varieties" and George White's "Scandals 1935". He staged the dances for Universal Pictures in "King of Jazz" and for 20th Century-Fox in "Moulin Rouge". Russell Markert shows are marked by original and eye-filling routines, rigorous precision, and by a superb blending of routines, costuming and lighting effects.

The talent world was combed for stars; a nation-wide call was sent out for beautiful girls with both skating and ballet training. Music was important, and they persuaded the Robbins Music Co. to assign capable young composers, Peter DeRose, John LaTouche and Mitchell Parish, to write the tunes that would fit the routines of the various skaters.

The entire organization assembled in Atlantic City on July 1, 1940, and with the facilities of the world's largest auditorium at their disposal, started two months of intensive training. The costumes were desgined by Willa Van and Michael Paul, and the entire staff of the big company of H. Mahieu, Inc. spent seven weeks making them.

And so, "Ice Capades of 1941" has born. It has been 38 years since the beginning of this great American organization, which showers on the public the supreme skating skill of the world.

The Costume and Design Dept. of Ice Capades discovered that they could save time and more importantly, money, if they costumed a doll before making the full size costumes. (Costuming is a vast part of the yearly expense of operating the Ice Capades). By dressing the dolls, they discover any errors that may happen, and can judge the materials to make sure they are water-proof, as well as durable and pliable. They can also "see" the finished costume. The dressing of the dolls to the completion of full sized costumes, is under the direction of Elizabeth Courtney, Director of the Ice Capades Costume Department. It takes more than 75 skilled tailors and dressmakers ten entire months to complete each year's costumes. The doll itself, was not important, just as long as it had an adult figure or look to it. Some of the dolls are composition, Alexander dolls, Kaysam, and even some Italian dolls were used. During the 1950's and early 1960's Cissy dolls were used, and later the Jacqueline doll was used.

After the Design and Costume Departments complete their work on the dolls, which is the result of a great amount of work and talent, the dolls are used by the Staging and Lighting Departments, who set up exact scale sets to help complete the details for the show. After all is completed, the dolls may be sent out on the road to make television appearances, to be set up as a display in a department store or in front of an arena. (The dolls are insured for up to $500.00). When the publicity tour is completed, the dolls are returned to the Ice Capades offices in Hollywood and put on display.

About 300 of the Ice Capade dolls were sold to one person, who has been re-selling them to dealers on the West Coast. There are just a few shown in this book, so that leaves a vast amount of them "out there" someplace. The non-Alexander dolls have been shown, so you can see the beauty of the costumes over the years.

From "Peter Pan" number of the 16″ Edition, 1956. The part of Peter Pan was played/skated by the world famous Donna Atwood. The doll's name was "Tiger Lily", and she was played by June Barlow. Doll is a Binnie Walker by Alexander.

18″ "Parisian Precision" from the 17″ Edition of the Ice Capades of 1958-1959. The doll used is an Italian one made by Furga. The entire number orginated and choreographed by Olympic Champions Rosemarie Stewart and Robert Dench.

I

20″ "Cavalcade of Hits" of the 19th Edition. 1959-1960. The doll is Cissy by Madame Alexander.

Ice Capades number "Bayaniman on Ice" of the 21st Edition 1961. Cissy doll by Madame Alexander.

This "My Fair Lady" number was performed by the Ice Capades during the 1962-1963 season (22nd Edition).

20″ "My Fair Lady". 22nd Edition 1962-1963. (Cissy)

This Ice Capades doll is from the 23rd Edition. 1963-64. "Rachmaninoff Concert" is the name of the number. Cissy doll by Madame Alexander.

20″ "Show Boat". 23rd Edition. 1963-1964. (Cissy)

20″ Cole Porter. 24th Edition. 1964-1965. (Cissy).

21″ "Precision". 25th Edition 1965-1966. (Jacqueline).

21″ Kaysam 1961 doll that is called "Seasons" and is from the 34th Edition of the Ice Capades in 1973-1974.

This is a photo from the 1971 program of Ice Capades and shows the finale "Tribute To The Age of Aquarius".

24″ This costume was used in the finale of the 31st Edition of Ice Capades of 1971 and called "Age of Aquarius". Marks: Kaysam 1961.

21″ "Sentimental Journey" number of the 33rd Edition of 1974, and called "Mombo". The doll is marked Kaysam 1961. The performers were Montaigne and Blake, Ann-Margaret Frei, along with the Ice Capets.

This 21″ doll was called "Reflections" and used in the opening number of the 34th Edition of Ice Capades in 1975. The doll is marked Kaysam 1961.

21″ "Gypsy Magic". From the 34th Edition of the Ice Capades of 1975. The skirt is removable. Marks: Kaysam 1961.

Shows the detail of the costume under the skirt.

21″ "Miss Judy's Grand Tour" exclusive with the FAO Schwarz stores in 1961. Brunette with brown eyes. In white satin gown with matching evening coat, pearl necklace, earrings and bag. She also wears rhinestone bracelets and a ring. 24″ metal trunk with pink taffeta cocktail dress with lace skirt panels and puffed sleeves, traveling suit of silk lined blue gabardine, corduroy slacks and jersey blouse, all-weather jacket, nylon tricot lace trimmed nightie and robe, hat and accessories. This outfit sold for $75.00 in 1962. All clothes may not be tagged Alexander. The stores often made up these trunks themselves. Tags on clothes can include "Debutante", "Halina's Doll Fashion", etc. The outfit worn by the dolls themselves should always have an Alexander tag.

21″ "Jacqueline" in outfit #2125-1962. This same outfit was sold through FAO Schwarz and Marshall Field. Brunette hair and brown eyes. (Courtesy Charmaine Shields)

The Marshall Field catalog of 1967 offered this 21″ Jacqueline as "Suzanne" with a handmade designer wardrobe in a Louis Vuitton trunk for $200.00. Gown is red, pantsuit white, and dress flair skirt deep blue.

This photo of Jane Withers was taken in 1936-1937 and appeared in a French magazine. Note the set of Alexander "Dionne Quints" and "Nurse" on the second shelf and the Effanbee dolls on the lower level, which include an "Ice Queen".

20″ "Jane Withers" with closed mouth. 1937. Pink dress with black tie and beret. This same dress came on open mouth versions also. It was thought, from the ads on the doll, that only the 13″ came with a closed mouth. Shown with an all original Shirley Temple. (18″) (Courtesy Sherry Kraft)

17″ Rare cloth body "Jane Withers". Brown mohair wig. The composition head is on a composition shoulderplate. Open mouth. Pink organdy dress has a Mollye label. Marks: Jane Withers/Alex. Doll Co., on head. 1937. Holds a 7½″ Lenci of 1930. (Courtesy Gloyra Woods)

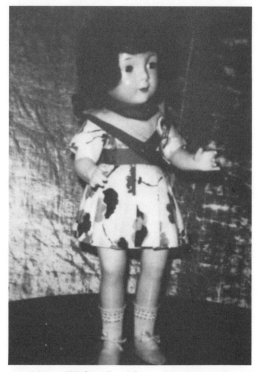

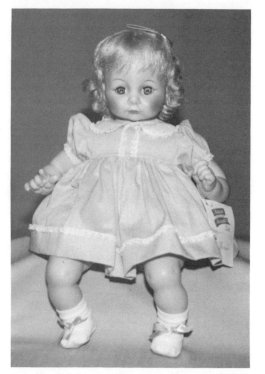

19″ "Jane Withers" with a closed mouth. All composition, brown sleep eyes and auburn mohair wig. Pin is not original. (Courtesy Mildred Hightower, photo by daughter, Cindy)

20″ "Janie" #5120-1972. Vinyl head and limbs on cloth body. Sleep eyes and rooted hair. **Marks:** Alexander/1971, on head. Sold during 1971-1973, only. (Courtesy Renie Culp)

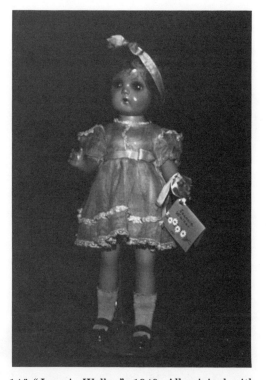

12″ "Janie Toddler" in white organdy dress with two tucks in skirt and lace trimmed yoke. Small blue and pink embroidered flowers on the yoke. Tag: Janie. #1156-1964. (Courtesy Kathleen Rudisill)

14″ "Jeannie Walker". 1940. All original with yellow organdy dress. 1941. (Courtesy Marge Meisinger)

14″ "Jeannie Walker". All composition with wood and composition walking mechanism. Sleep eyes and closed, puckered mouth. All original. Marks: Alexander/Pat. N. 2171281, on back. Tag: Madame/Alexander/New York, N.Y. This same tag is on the pink organdy dress under coat. #1690-1942. (Courtesy Gloyra Woods)

14″ John Powers Model. (Maggie). All hard plastic and original with black hat box. (Courtesy Karen Conlay)

36″ "Joanie" #3518-1960. Plastic with vinyl head and arms. Flirting, sleep eyes. Rooted hair, which came in various colors and styles. Second and third fingers molded together on right hand, all others molded separately. All original. (Courtesy Doris Richardson)

36″ "Joannie Nurse and Baby" were offered through catalogs during 1960. Plastic with vinyl head, flirting eyes. The 1960 cost was $24.98.

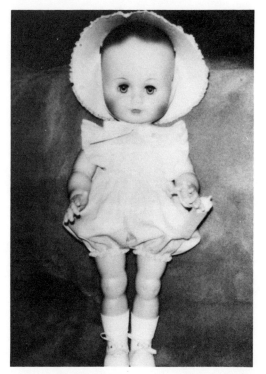

23″ "Kathleen" #7924-1959. New shoes and socks. This doll also came with molded hair and a variation of this dress. (#7824-1959)(Courtesy Doris Richardson)

23″ "Kathleen" #7820-1959. All vinyl with blue sleep eyes and molded hair. Original. Pink romper suit and matching bonnet. (Courtesy Doris Richardson)

"Kathy" dressed in two-tone cotton trimmed in contrasting rick-rack. Beret of black velvet and patent leather slippers with white socks. The doll came in sizes 15″, 18″ and 23″ in this outfit in the 1951 FAO Schwarz catalog. It was #1515-1952 and 1953. (Maggie). The "Annabelle" shown in Vol. I, page 93 is really a "Kathy". (Courtesy Roberta Lago)

18″ "Kathy". 1951. All hard plastic with light blonde saran wig in pigtails. Blue sleep eyes. All original outfit of clan tartan pedal-pushers, red corduroy wesket, over sheer white blouse and Scotch tam with red feather. Brown oxford roller skates. Has small basket charm. Tag: Mme Alexander N.Y./All rights reserved. (Maggie) (Courtesy Rita DiMare)

The 11″ size, all vinyl open mouth/nurser baby, "Kathy" came in a window-boxed package with layette. 1957-1958. Catalog reprint.

"Kathy" of 1958 came in 11″, 15″, 18″, 21″ and 25″ in this outfit. Organdy dress with baby coat trimmed with lace and pearl buttons. Matching bonnet with double frill of lace on nylon tulle. Catalog reprint.

12″ "Kathy" #622-1954. All vinyl, drinks and wets. In original sunsuit and bonnet. Dark pink and white waffle-type material trimmed with white rick-rack and lace. Marks: Alexander, on head. (Courtesy Kathleen Rudisill)

"Kathy Tears" came in 11″, 17″, 19″ sizes in 1960. All vinyl, drinks and wets and cries tears. Molded hair and also wigged. Romper of checkered cotton with matching bonnet, lace trimmed.

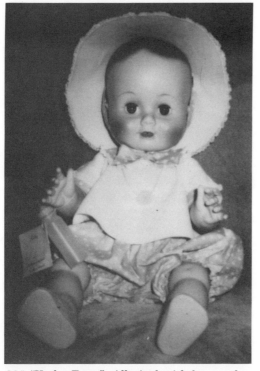

23″ "Kathy Tears". All vinyl with brown sleep eyes and molded hair. #6805-1959. This romper also came in checkered. (Courtesy Doris Richardson)

"Kathy Tears" came in this layette box in the 12″ size only. 1961. All vinyl baby, drinks and wets. Romper is checkered cotton trimmed with lace.

This two-piece dress and over-dress were sold extra in 1957 for all size Kellys. 12″, 16″ and 22″. (Courtesy Linda Crowsey)

12″ "Kelly" of 1959. Matches other Kellys of that year. All hard plastic with extra joints. Note earrings that are pierced into the head and have glue added. One piece satin panties and half slip that is organdy with net and lace. (Lissy) Tag: Kelly/Madame Alexander /Reg. US Pat. Off. NY USA. (Courtesy Marge Meisinger)

12″ "Kelly" #1103-1959. Yellow nylon dress with two rows of ruffles around the neck, and one row around the arms. Black shoes and ribbon. Tag: Kelly/Madame Alexander, etc. (Courtesy Barbara Schilde)

"Kelly" was introduced in 1958 and came in various outfits. 15″ and 22″ size came in this plain polished cotton with striped pinafore. (Marybel). Catalog reprint.

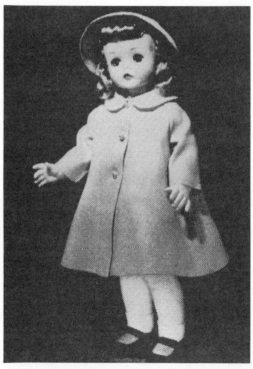

22″ "Kelly". (Marybel). Hard plastic and vinyl. Jointed waist. In pink vinyl raincoat and hat lined with white with blue polka dots. #1924-1958. Marks: Alexander, on head. At shoulders has unusual marks: (MME 1958 ALEX.), then has usual mark low on back: (MME 19©58 ALEXANDER) (Courtesy Janine Chatstrom)

16″ & 22″ "Kelly" came with this wool coat, fully lined and worn over a nylon dress. Milan straw hat. 1958. Catalog reprint.

16″ & 22″ "Kelly" of 1958 came in this dress that was nylon with lots of lace trim. Came in various colors. Catalog reprint.

This catalog reprint (Wards-1959) shows 16″ "Kelly" and 12″ "Kelly". (Lissy). Both are dressed in strawberry pink taffeta dress with overdress of lace trimmed organdy. Pink straw hat and tiny tourqouise earrings.

This "Kelly Takes a Trip" was an exclusive for the FAO Schwarz stores in 1959. 16″ doll wears a blue nylon dress with pleated skirt and ribbon trimmed straw hat. Trunk is 18″ tall. White cotton nightie with embroidered yoke, striped cotton robe, flowered bathing suit, blue ballet outfit with matching slippers and pink polished cotton street dress, pearls, mirror, comb, brush, earrings and purse. This doll in trunk sold for $38.50.

21″ "Kitten". Cloth and vinyl, rooted white hair, blue sleep eyes. White organdy dress with lace and tucks. Satin ribbon flowers of several colors at bodice line. Pink knit booties. Marks: Alexander 1961, on head. Tag: Kitten #6520-1961, although the catalog listed this doll as 24″ tall. (Courtesy Kathleen Rudisill)

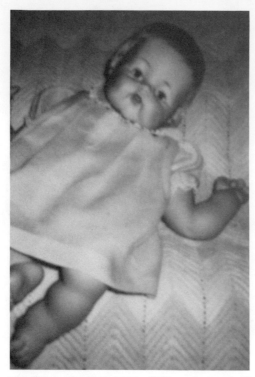

24″ "Kitten" #6510-1961. Cloth and vinyl with rooted hair and sleep eyes. Excellent toe and finger detail. (Courtesy Doris Richardson)

14″ "Lively Kitten Trousseau" in 16″ case. Eight piece layette. The case is pink. Sold in the 1962 FAO Schwarz catalog for $16.95.

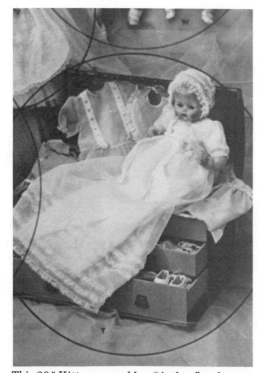

This 20″ Kitten was sold as "Andrea" and was an exclusive at Marshall-Field in 1969. She had 12 outfits (ad says "many of which have hand detail). The trunk is a Napoleanic dome-top by Louis Vuitton of Paris. This doll/trunk cost $395.00 in 1969.

17″ "Leslie" #1632-1965. Plastic and vinyl. (Polly-Maria). All original, except she had roses at waist. This doll is being sold as "Leslie Uggums", and this is incorrect. The doll was never meant to be Miss Uggums. (Courtesy Mary Partridge)

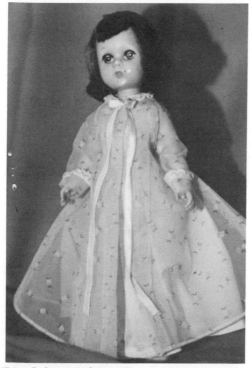

"Lissy" shown in her pink gown and sheer green pegnoir with flocking. #1220-1956. Tag: Lissy, etc. (Courtesy Linda Crowsey)

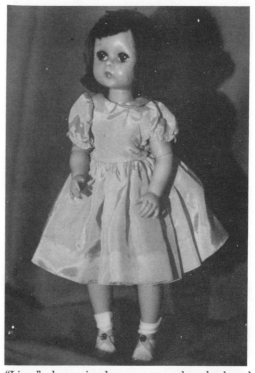

"Lissy" shown in dress worn under checkered coat lined in same material as dress. With straw hat (missing). Came in various pastel colors. This is #1233-1956, and is yellow taffeta. Doll has extra joints. (Courtesy Linda Crowsey)

12″ "Lissy" with pig-tails. #1237-1956. Pink taffeta dress, rick-rack trim and feather stitching on bodice and hem. Navy coat. All original. (Courtesy Beth Donar)

"Lissy" dressed in #1230-1956. Candy striped red and white two-piece dress, blouse and skirt with white lace trim. (Courtesy Deedee Shields)

12″ "Lissy" in #1241-1956. Aqua blue organdy with feather-stitch trim and lace. This dress also came in white, yellow, pink and blue. (Courtesy Roberta Lago)

"Lissy" and wardrobe sold for $15.95 from the FAO Schwarz catalog in 1956. Lissy came dressed in a chimese of swiss eyelet embroidery, strap sandals and socks. Her nine piece wardrobe, included silk nightie, nylon robe, coat and hat, taffeta dress, petticoat, panties, curlers, shoes and a plastic barrette. The box has a clear plastic window.

12″ "Lissy" dressed in #1225-1956 called "Afternoon Tea". Pink taffeta and lace with pink straw hat. Also listed as "Southern Belle" 1956. (Courtesy Roberta Lago)

12″ Lissy Ballerina in pink #1242-1956 as the "Sugar Plum Fairy" (in pink only). #1214-1957 and 1958 were in white mostly and some in blue. This one wears pink nylon tights. (Courtesy Beth Donar)

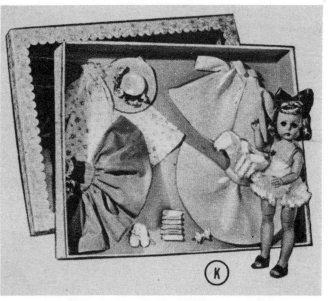

"Lissy" and her wardrobe were sold through FAO Schwarz in 1957 and sold for $15.95. Doll is dressed in lace trimmed nylon chimese, strap sandals and long nylon hose. Included in the window box package were nine items, nylon robe, pink coat and hat with matching swing skirt and lace trimmed nylon blouse, taffeta dress, curlers, mules and a plastic barrette.

Lissy as "Bride" #1247-1956. All original. (Courtesy Linda Crowsey)

"Lissy" is shown in her original case with extra clothes as sold at FAO Schwarz-1956. In 1957, she was packaged in this same wardrobe trunk, but the long dress she is wearing was made without the lace on the skirt. The doll with the red dress was offered in 1957 in a "window-box" package. (Courtesy Deedee Shields)

12" "Lissy" #1151-1957. Jointed elbows and knees. All hard plastic. Wide pilgrim collar is detachable. Tag: Lissy. (Courtesy Bessie Carson)

12" "Lissy Bridesmaid". #1161-1957. Blue nylon dress and hat with nylon chiffon tie. Lace trim on skirt. This item also included in trunk. (Courtesy Pat Spirek)

"Lissy" wears a pink checkered dress with an organdy apron style pinafore. #1164-1957. (Courtesy Linda Crowsey)

12" "Lissy" in a short party dress of lace trimmed sheer dotted nylon, satin ribbon sash and flower trimmed hat. 1957. #1167. Catalog reprint.

12" "Lissy" dressed in #1217-1958. Red cotton dress and organdy pinafore with feather-stitching. (Courtesy Barbara Schilde)

12″ "Lissy" in #1218-1958. Checkered dress with trimmed cotton pinafore. Straw hat with flowers missing. (Courtesy Linda Crowsey)

12″ "Lissy" #1222-1958. Hard plastic with jointed knees. Jointed elbows. Sleep blue eyes, blonde wig. Red and white dress of cotton. Tag: Lissy Madame Alexander. (Courtesy Sharon Ivy)

12″ "Lissy" #1210-1958 in organdy party dress, lace trimmed taffeta underwear, long nylon hose, strap sandals and a straw hat trimmed with flowers. Catalog reprint.

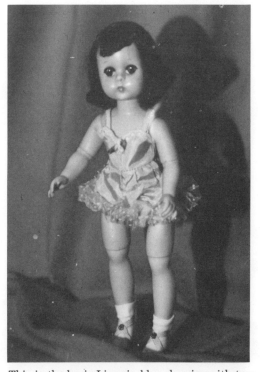

This is the basic Lissy in blue chemise with tag: Lissy. Extra joints at elbows and knees. Replaced shoes. #1200-1958. (Courtesy Linda Crowsey)

12″ "McGuffey Ana" of the Lissy Classic group. #1258-1963. Red velvet suit with circular lined skirt and jacket, deep pile white fur-like hat, coat collar and mittens. Long white stockings, patent leather slippers and buttoned gaitors (spats). Hair in pigtails.

12″ "Lissy Classic Southern Belle". #1255. Hard plastic with extra joints. Blue taffeta with lace trim. 1963. In 1964 there was a matching 8″ Southern Belle. (See Alexander-kin section). (Courtesy Susan Goetz)

12″ Lissy "Cinderella" #1240 in gift box. Gown on doll is pale blue satin, trimmed with lace, sequins and rosebuds. Other dress is moss green with kerchief, bright orange apron and broom. The Lissy was also available in each outfit by itself. 1966. Catalog reprint.

12″ Lissy Classic Cinderella. #1240-1966. Sold separately and also came in gift set. This angle shows the length of the hairdo.

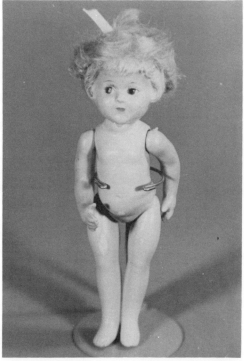

11½" "Little Audrey". 1954. One-piece stuffed vinyl body and limbs. Wood neck plug. Deep "V" impressed into lower back. Alexander, on head. Early vinyl head with molded hair under wig. Wig is parted in middle in back, with short cluster curls to side tied with red ribbon, top hair pulled back on sides and tied at top with ribbon. Painted black eyes. Panties attached to dress. Replaced shoes and socks. Tag: Little Audrey/Madame Alexander/New York USA. (Courtesy Marjorie Uhl)

8½" "Little Colonel". 1935. All composition with smile and dimples. Brown painted eyes to side. Molded hair under wig. This is replaced wig, and doll has painted brown hair under it, so is likely to have been marketed without a wig. Bent right arm. Thumb is only finger that is separate. Marks: A.D. Co., on head. Alexander, on back. (Courtesy Marge Meisinger)

24" Open mouth "Little Colonel". All composition with brown sleep eyes and all original. Pale pink and pale blue organdy dress and bonnet, white undies and pantaloons. No marks on the doll. Tag: Madame Alexander Presents "Little Colonel"/Trademark Alexander doll Company N.Y. This is apparently a "pre" Princess Elizabeth head. (Courtesy Sue Austin)

Original paper wrist tag on "Little Colonel" doll. (Courtesy Sue Austin)

13″ "Little Colonel". All composition with mohair wig, blue tin sleep eyes, closed mouth and dimples. Doll is unmarked. Tag: Madame Alexander/New York. 1935. Shown with 17″ Alexander that is re-dressed. (Courtesy Glorya Woods)

14″ "Little Colonel" of 1935 and 1936. All composition and original. Doll is not marked, and the dress is tagged: Madame Alexander. Closed mouth and cheek dimples. Blue sleep eyes. (Courtesy Pat Spirek)

27″ "Little Colonel" of 1935. All composition with brown sleep eyes, open mouth and slight cheek dimples. All original. (Courtesy Marjorie Uhl)

17″ "Little Genius". Laytex arms and legs, cloth body and hard plastic head. Tag: Little Genius/Madame Alexander, N.Y. U.S.A./All Rights Reserved. (Courtesy Lillian Roth)

16½″ "Little Genius". Hard plastic head, cloth body and vinyl limbs. 1950. Reddish mohair wig over molded hair. Pale yellow organdy dress and bonnet. Pink slip and panties. Blue shoes. Tag: Little Genius by Madame Alexander. (Courtesy Sharon Ivy)

"Little Genius" in christening outfit #235-1959. (Courtesy Loramay Wilson)

Baby Little Genius #104-1958. Had jacket with one button at neck and collar. #105-1958 came in striped material, but same. (Courtesy Barbara Schilde)

8″ "Little Genius" in outfit #147-1958. (Courtesy Loramay Wilson)

L

This sewing basket and 8″ "Little Genius" was an exclusive in 1960 FAO Schwarz catalog. The wicker basket is 5½″ x 6½″ x 9″. The doll has on checkered panties. The other outfits are ready to sew. The cost was $7.95 in 1960.

H 3-122 SEWING BASKET (Exclusive) S (7 yrs. up)—A 5½″ x 6½″ x 9″ wicker bo carrying handle, containing thimble, sciss ~~of pearl buttons, needle book, pin cushic~~

1959 FAO Schwarz catalog. Sewing basket exclusive with 8″ "Little Genius" dressed only in panties. Basket is 5½″ x 6½″ x 9″.

"Little Genius" in overalls is #221-1961, and the dress is a boxed extra outfit sold in 1960 (#0230). (Courtesy Loramay Wilson)

This 1964 sewing basket set was also sold in 1965 and cost $9.95 from the FAO Schwarz catalog. Has five complete outfits for the 8″ "Little Genius". Each outfit is cut and ready to sew; trim and instructions were included. 5½″ x 6½″ x 9″ wicker basket with handle contains thimble, thread, scissors, needle book and pin cushion. The basket is narrower at the top than at the bottom.

7½" "Little Madaline" of 1953. Straight-leg non-walker. This is a miniature of the dress used on one of the larger sized Madalines. (Courtesy Marge Meisinger)

7" "Little Red Riding Hood". (Tiny Betty). All composition with painted on shoes and socks and painted eyes. All original. 1936-1940. (Courtesy Marge Meisinger)

Madame Alexander (left) is shown with Elsie Shaver, the originator of the Victorian Children painting. Also shown are two sizes of "Little Shaver" dolls by Madame Alexander. 1937.

#2930-1963. "Little Shaver". Original with white organdy panties with lace trim. Painted eyes. Marks: Mme. Alexander, in circle on head. Tag: Little Shaver. (Courtesy Linda Crowsey)

13" "Little Shaver Baby". All cloth and in original taffeta dress with lace trim and matching bonnet. Thin yarn hair curls away from the face. This doll differs from the 1930's "So-lite" dolls in that the face is almost round and "flatter", the eyes are larger and much more round and not as painted "to the side" as the So-Lite dolls. 1939-40.

7½" "Amy" of the Little Women. All composition, jointed at shoulders only. Painted on shoes and socks. Mohair blonde wig, painted eyes to the side. Original clothes. Marks: Alex., on back. Amy M. Alexander, on dress tag. 1936-1939. (Courtesy A. P. Miller)

LITTLE WOMEN - LOUISA MAY ALCOTT

Louisa May Alcott wrote the 'Little Women' at the age of 35 in an attempt to please her father, Bronson Alcott, who was a famous philosopher and educator. Bronson Alcott was a close friend and companion of authors Emerson and Thoreau. Mr. Alcott regarded contemplation as an occupation, and allowed his wife and three of their four daughters to support him for most of his lifetime.

It was in May of 1868 that Louisa May Alcott began her novel, "Little Women" against her own protest. Her father had been trying to get her to write a story directed at a young audience, telling the story of triumph of goodness and all-forgiving love over the flaws of selfishness and anger. Louisa had attempted her entire life to subdue these very things within herself and felt no need to write about the problems. But when her publisher also suggested that she write a book for girls, she gave in; plus the family pocketbook needed a boost, as usual.

So, seated at her writing desk under her bedroom window, Louisa began. She even amazed herself that first day of writing, for she continued to write all day, and never rethinking nor rewriting a word, she liked the story she was putting on paper. She finished the manuscript in July, 1868, and upon reading the entire thing, felt it was dull. Her publisher agreed but 2,000 copies sold out immediately. The publisher asked for a second volume, and in November, 1868 Louisa began writing the sequel, which she finished in January of 1869. By August of this same year, Louisa May Alcott was as well known as an author of the day could have been.

Louisa May was born in 1832, and was the second daughter of Bronson and Abba Alcott. From the time she was born, Louisa was naughty and considered a trouble-maker with a firey temper. Even the passive father admitted that Louisa disturbed him. Louisa tried, and managed after many years, to supress her anger, dispair and disappointments. She had been born into a situation where the men exchanged elevated conversations while Abba Alcott and the four girls rose at 5 A.M. to wash, cook, iron and clean for the talkers. The Alcotts lived miserably, depending on charity from relatives and friends, and as the family grew, upon the income of the girls. The girls worked as governesses, nursemaids, servants and schoolmarms. Through all this, Louisa came to the conclusion that marriage was not "wedded bliss". Louisa became determined not to ever have to depend upon a man, and she turned more and more into her world of fantasy and her writings.

When the Civil War started, Louisa went to Washington to help nurse the wounded. She was 30. Louisa became seriously ill with typhoid pneumonia and nearly died. As a result of her illness, she suffered from doses of calomel, the source of mercury poisoning, and had to depend on opium and morphine the rest of her life to ease the pain of her body. She spent the rest of her life taking care of her family, who had become dependent upon her strength and talents. She died a spinster at age 55.

In the novel "Little Women" Louisa's real sister Anna was Meg, Elizabeth was Beth, May was Amy and, of course, Louisa herself, was Jo.

There were so many sets of 14"-15" hard plastic Little Women, and so many variations of the same sets, that it is difficult to pin-point all of them as to year. The following sets have been found in ads.

8″ "Meg" of Little Women. 1936-1939. All composition with painted eyes to side and painted on shoes and socks. Tag: Meg Madame Alexander, etc. (Courtesy Barbara Schilde)

1949-1950 Little Women. Top: Left to right: "Meg" and "Marme". Center: "Beth". Bottom row left to right: "Jo" and "Amy". (Courtesy Roberta Lago)

Back view of Little Women of 1949-1950. Note curls at nape of neck on "Amy". (Courtesy Roberta Lago)

Late 1948-1949 set of 15″ Little Women. Margaret-face "Amy" with rope curls, "Meg" is a Margaret-face doll with red/white stripe dress and attached apron, "Marme" has the Margaret face (center), "Jo" has the Maggie face with red dress and black yoke, and "Beth" has the Maggie face with dress of pink, blue, purple grey, peach and green stripe with attached white apron. (Courtesy Beth Donor)

This set of 14″ Little Women was shown in 1952 and is (A) "Meg"; (B) "Jo"; (C) "Marme"; (D) "Amy" and (E) "Beth". (Margaret and Maggie). All hard plastic. The dolls cost $50.00 a set in 1952 ($10.00 each).

Shows set of 1952 Little Women. Left to right: "Meg" (has different apron than shown in the FAO Schwarz catalog of 1952) "Beth", "Marme" and "Jo". "Amy" is in background. (Courtesy Mary Partridge)

14″ "Meg" from the 1951 set of Little Women. The dress is blue dotted Swiss with attached white apron. Dark blonde hair with braid over the top. This same doll also came with a fine polka dot dress. (Courtesy Rita DiMare)

14″ "Amy" (Margaret) from the 1952 set of Little Women. Pink taffeta flowered dress and tagged Amy. Variation of print used must be noted from the 1953 set. (Courtesy Carole Nori)

Back of the 1952 "Amy" to show the loose curls around nape of neck. (Courtesy Carole Nori)

15″ "Jo" from the 1951 set of Little Women. The gown is a deep red taffeta with black "bib". (Courtesy Mary Partridge)

This is a group of Little Women advertised in the FAO Schwarz catalog during 1953. 15″ tall, all hard plastic and cost $10.00 each. Note two have the large hands and three the small hands. (B) "Meg"; (C) "Beth"; (D) "Marme"; (E) "Jo"; (F) "Amy". ("Beth" and "Amy" have the large hands)

8″ "Marme". Brown print cotton with white bib collar, black taffeta half apron. Variation of print of 1954. Tag: Alexander-kins Marme. Matches 15″ "Marme" of 1954. (Courtesy Dave and Kathy Ethington)

This is the 8″ set of Little Women of 1955.

These 15″ Little Women are all hard plastic and have the large hands. 1955, and from an FAO Schwarz catalog. They were $50.00 a set ($10.00 each). (K) "Meg"; (L) "Jo"; (M) "Amy"; (N) "Marme" and (P) "Beth".

This Margaret faced, all hard plastic "Amy" is from the 1955 set of Litte Women and shows a variation of print used. The doll is 14-15″ tall. (Courtesy Loramay Wilson)

This is the 1956 set of Little Women. They are 15″ tall and all hard plastic. (Margaret & Maggie). (C) "Meg"; (D) "Jo"; (E) "Marme"; (F) "Beth"; (G) "Amy". All have large hands.

8″ 1958 set of Little Women using the Wendy/Alexander-kin dolls. "Jo" in polished cotton with white organdy blouse. "Meg" in blue striped pinafore. "Amy" in lace trimmed print. "Beth" in checked cotton and "Marme" in plaid taffeta with taffeta apron and fichu of organdy. Set #581.

The 1957 Alexander catalog shows this set of Little Women in the 8″ size.

11½″ "Amy" of Little Women (Lissy). Set #1225-1958. Dress had a variation of different prints used. Jointed elbows and knees. Tag: Louisa M. Alcott's/Little Women Amy/by Madame Alexander N.Y., U.S.A./All rights reserved. (Courtesy Jackie Barker)

1959 Lissy Little Women as shown in the 1959 FAO Schwarz catalog. (M) "Amy"; (N) "Jo"; (P) "Meg"; (R) "Marme"; (S) "Beth".

12″ Lissy Little Women. (M) "Meg"; (N) "Beth"; (P) "Marme"; (R) "Jo"; (L) "Amy." From the 1960 FAO Schwarz catalog.

The 1959 Alexander catalog lists both the 8″ and 12″ sets of Little Women. This is the 12″ using the Lissy.

8″ "Jo" with bending knees. 1960. Blue with red apron. Matches the larger "Jo". (Courtesy Renie Culp)

12″ "Jo" of Little Women using the Lissy doll. #1125-1960. The apron is red. (Courtesy Lilah M. Beck)

12″ "Meg" of Little Women using the Lissy doll. #1225-1961. (Courtesy Lilah M. Beck)

12″ Lissy Little Women from the 1962 FAO Schwarz catalog. (M) "Marme"; (N) "Meg"; (P) "Jo"; (R) "Amy"; (S) "Beth".

The 1965 Lissy Little Women from the FAO Schwarz catalog are: (B) "Amy"; (C) "Meg"; (D) "Beth"; (E) "Jo"; (F) "Marme".

This "Lissy" used as the "Laurie" for the last 12″ sets of Little Women is a rare and difficult doll to find. "Lissy" 1957 to 1967. "Laurie" 1967 only. 8″ "Laurie" added in 1966. (Courtesy Marge Meisinger)

12″ "Marme" (Lissy). This dress and apron first appeared in 1962, but the early ones do not have the two rows of lace on the bodice, nor white cuffs on the sleeves. #1225-1965. (Courtesy Barbara Schilde)

12″ "Jo". #1225-1969. Matches the 8″ one. Doll is marked Alexander/1963, on head. Plastic and vinyl (Nancy Drew). (Courtesy Renie Culp)

12″ "Laurie", who is marked Alexander/1963, on head. Has older checkered pants. (Nancy Drew) (Courtesy Renie Culp)

12″ "Marme" with two rows of lace on front. Doll is marked Alexander 1963, on head. (Nancy Drew) (Courtesy Renie Culp)

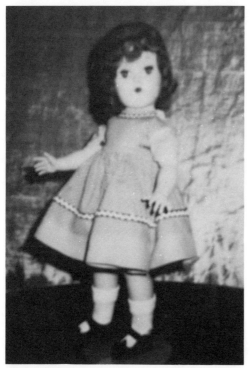

15½" "Looby Loo". All hard plastic using the Snow White (Compo) head. Red mohair wig and blue sleep eyes. All fingers spread. Closed mouth. Cotton blue and white dotted dress with red trim, over-trimmed with white rick-rack. Dress label reads: Looby Loo Madame Alexander/New York U.S.A. Ca. 1951-1954. The following trademark is only thing we have been able to find on this doll: Jan. 10, 1950 #545,632 Looby Loo Designers, Minniapolis, Minn. To use "Looby Loo" for dolls, clothes and furniture. (Courtesy Mildred Hightower, photo by daughter, Cindy)

8" "Littlest Kitten" #530-1963. One-piece red leotard and pique pinafore with rick-rack on collar and sleeves. Grape applique. All vinyl with bent baby legs. Sleep eyes. Marks; Alex. Doll Co., on head. (Courtesy Bessie Carson)

8" "Littlest Kitten" #551-1963. All vinyl with rooted hair. (Courtesy Carrie Perkins)

8" "Littlest Kitten" in #845-1964. The dress is pink and white checkered, with white lace trim, and she wears a pink ribbon in her hair. (Courtesy Linda Crowsey)

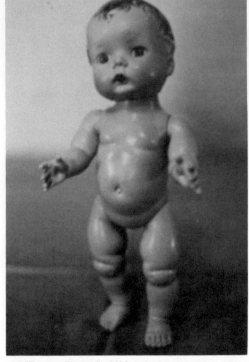

12″ "Lovey Dovey". All hard plastic with molded hair, sleep eyes and much detail on body. Toddler. This doll is shown in the 1948 Sears catalog with eight piece layette in a wicker basket, open at the top and with loop handles. (Courtesy Janine Chalstrom)

1958 introduced 19″ "Lovey Dovey". One outfit she came in is this romper of checkered gingham with an edge of lace and a small white collar. Matching bonnet. Catalog reprint.

19″ "Lovey Dovey" #5920-1958. All vinyl with rooted hair. Also in 1958 this same doll came with this outfit, but had molded hair (#5820). All original. (Courtesy Doris Richardson)

7½″ "Madaline". (Wendy). 1953. Tag: Made for Neiman Marcus, styled after Ludwig Bemelman Rhymed Stories about "Madeline the Parisian Orphan". (Courtesy Mary Williams)

MADALINE

Madaline was a very successful doll made by the Alexander Doll Company in the early 1950's. She was built on an old (yet new to that generation) concept because the doll was fully jointed, could bend her elbows, twist her wrists and kneel. The doll's wardrobe was among the most beautiful and plentiful ever made for any doll. Madaline was an all hard plastic doll with an early vinyl head, open/closed mouth and sleep eyes. (Used also for the Sonja Henie doll but Madaline was a "rich girl's" doll.) Let's look at some of the descriptions that came with the doll.

First the doll, Madaline, is owned by a little girl, Lucy. Here is one paragraph describing "One Fine Morning". "This is marketing day for cook, and she has promised to take Lucy to market. Lucy loves to go . . . here comes the chauffeur with the car . . . cook is all ready and waiting for Lucy, who is skipping down the garden path. You can be sure she is bringing Madaline." One caption that is under a taffeta raincoat describes Lucy and Madaline getting ready to go to an Orphan Home to take baskets of gifts. Under pictures of Madaline dressed in a slack set or three-piece play suit is the caption "Madaline Goes to a Picnic" . . . "They watch cook unpack the wonderful baskets for Madaline's picnic." Another caption is titled "Television until Eight" "Daddy is away tonight so Mummy and Lucy and Madaline have supper served before the fire in the library".

Madaline may have been a rich girl's doll, but when a less than rich girl was lucky enough to get one of the dolls (basic price in 1951 was $12.95) she loved it as much, and perhaps dreamed that she was that little girl who had a cook, chauffeur and a library in her home.

MADALINE DOLL—One of the most beautiful of all dolls. Madaline is . . . of the very finest hard plastic, tinted to look life-

Clothes for the Madaline doll of 1953, sold from the FAO Schwarz catalog. (D) White organdy party dress trimmed with organdy ruffles, edged with red rick-rack. (Cost then: $7.95); (E) Bolero dress in red polished cotton. (Cost then: $3.00); (F) Raincoat and hat of striped taffeta in red and white or blue and white. (Cost then: $3.00); (G) Pink organdy dress with insets of Swiss embroidery. (Cost then: $5.00).

This is an 18″ "Madaline" and wardrobe that was in the ads of the Nov. 1952 House and Garden Magazine. The doll sold for $19.95 and could be ordered from the Dayton Co. The clothes ran from $1.50 to $6.00 each.

16½″ "Madeline". Kelly faced/Elise body with jointed ankles and elbows. Rooted hair in vinyl head. Dark brown hair and blue sleep eyes. Shoes not original. 1964. Tag: Madaline Madame Alexander, etc. (Courtesy Sharon Ivy)

14″ "Madeleine de Baines". All hard plastic (Maggie). Dark brown mohair wig in double row of curls across the back and one roll curl across the back of the head. Blue-green sleep eyes. White cotton dress printed with roses and ruffle at hem. Black velvet bows and trim. Lace on yoke. Tag: Madeleine de Bains/Madame Alexander/All Rights Reserved. 1949. There was a 15″ and a 17″ in this same dress. On the 17″ size the dress came to just below the knees. (Courtesy Sharon Ivy)

14″ "Maggie" and her trousseau sold at FAO Schwarz in 1951 for $21.95. Dressed in a gaberdine skirt with kick pleats and white shirt. Brown/white saddle shoes. Wardrobe includes 28 pieces.

15″ "Maggie Teenager". (#1517) All hard plastic. Blue/white striped blouse with shirt waist front and buttons. Shirt is red, saddle shoes are tied and brown/white. Attached chain at waist holds same basket as on the Godey Lady of 1949. 1950-1951. Tag: Madame Alexander, etc. (Courtesy Charmaine Shields)

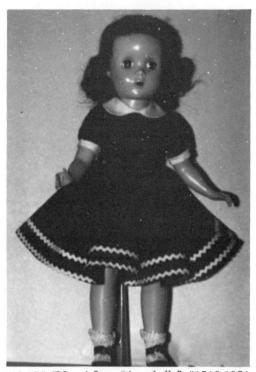

15″ "Maggie Walker Trousseau" of 1952, which sold for $20.00, at FAO Schwarz is identical to Annabelle Trousseau of the same year.

14″-15″ "Maggie" or "Annabelle" #1510-1951. This is the Annabelle dress without the sweater of a contrasting color, but it is not known if the Maggie was sold with the dress only. (Courtesy Loramay Wilson)

20″ "Maggie Walker". All hard plastic with red wig. Skirt, blouse and wide contour belt. #2016-1952. (Courtesy Sherry Kraft)

14″ "Maggie Walker". All hard plastic with golden hair and brown eyes. Pink dotted swiss dress. #1518-1952. (Courtesy Beth Donar)

17″ "Maggie Walker" #1813-1952. All hard plastic with red wig. Sleeveless dress with white pique top and pleated mauve rayon skirt. Wool sweater that was white, but turned yellow with passing time. Taffeta panties and half slip with lace edging. Carries box with comb and curlers. Doll unmarked. Tag: Madame Alexander/New York U.S.A. (Courtesy Ambri Cardenas)

15″ "Maggie Walker" in #1516-1953. Pink embossed cotton dress. All original. It must be noted that this same material was used for a dress for the American Character Sweet Sue doll. (Courtesy Loramay Wilson)

8″ "Maggie Mix-up" (Wendy). Bend-knee walker. Pink/white stripe leotard under green felt skirt with pink felt flowers and rhinestone centers. #356-1957. Pixie hat missing, as well as roller skates. (Courtesy Dave and Kathy Ethington)

8″ "Maggie Mixup". Bend-knee walker with red hair, green eyes, smile mouth and freckles. Wears blue and white print apron with rick-rack trim over red cotton dress and red bonnet. Dress tagged: Maggie Madame Alexander. #594-1960. (Courtesy Dave and Kathy Ethington)

8″ "Maggie Mixup" in #599-1960 with tag: Maggie. Yellow cotton dress with attached print apron. Pink taffeta panties with bows. Panties are also tagged Maggie. (Courtesy Linda Crowsey)

8″ #599-1960 "Maggie Mixup" with a variation of color and print of apron. Yellow cotton sleeveless dress with lavender print apron. Bend-knee walker. Red, straight Maggie wig, blue sleep eyes and freckles. This is the standard Wendy-Alexander-kin head, yet has the freckles and hair of the Maggie Mix-up. The doll is mint and original. (Courtesy Pat Spirek)

8″ "Maggie Mix-up" of 1960 in red ribbed slacks with gold waistband, white knit blouse and red felt hat with black pom-pom. Tag: Maggie. Bend-knee walker. (Courtesy Bernice Heister)

This "Maggie Mix-up on Tour" was an exclusive for FAO Schwarz in 1960. 16″ and in a 18″ trunk. She wears a party dress of soft pink cotton with organdy top and velvet sash, straw hat, nylon hose, flat slippers and necklace. This same doll and dress were sold separately for $12.95 and the trousseau cost $42.95. Also included were full skirted blue evening gown with underskirt and hooped petticoat, high heeled slipper, stockings, purse, comb, brush and mirror, two-piece slack set, crepe nightie, lace robe and wool coat with matching hat.

This is a close-up of the faces of a Wendy-Alexander-kin, 1957 and the Wendy-faced "Maggie Mixup", 1961. (Courtesy Kathy Ethington)

17″ "Maggie Mix-up" #1855-1961. This doll was made for just two years. Straight red hair and sleep blue or green eyes. All original, except hat is missing (see other photo). There is a variation of skirt trim. (Courtesy Charmaine Shield)

8″ "Maggie Mixup" #610-1961. Holds plastic watering can. Straight red hair, freckles and green sleep eyes. (Courtesy Sherry Kraft)

1977 21″ Portrait "Magnolia". #2297. Head is marked 1961, as all the Portraits are. (Courtesy Renie Culp)

21″ "Margaret O'Brien". All composition. Marked: Alexander on head and Madame Alexander on body. Variation of the same dress used on the 18″ size in 1946-1947. From the movie "Calling All Girls". (Courtesy Pat Spirek)

18″ "Margaret O'Brien". All composition with reddish mohair wig and blue sleep eyes. All original. Marks: Alexander, on head and body. Tag: Madame/Alexander/New York, N.Y. 1946. (Courtesy Glorya Woods)

21″ "Margaret O'Brien", gowned from the movie "Meet Me In St. Louis", when she co-starred with Judy Garland. All composition. The gown is off-white and ribbons are grosgrain type with rose flowers. Mohair wig. Tag: Madame Alexander/All Rights Reserved, etc. 1946.

14″ "Margaret Rose" (Princess). 1953. All hard plastic and a mint and original doll. (Margaret). Pink gown with purse to match and straw hat with flowers and bows. Tag: Margaret Rose Madame Alexander NY/All Rights Reserved. Green clover tag on wrist: Madame Alexander. (Courtesy Rosemary Meyecic)

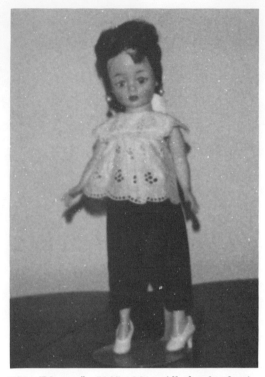

21″ "Margaret Rose". All composition. Yellow net gown and flowers with natural straw hat and yellow flowers. (Margaret). All original and tagged Margaret Rose. 1946. (Courtesy Marge Meisinger)

10″ "Margot" #905-1961. All hard plastic. (Cissette). Has more eye makeup than the regular Cissettes with blue eye lids. Elaborate hairdo. Black pants with white top. (Courtesy Sandra Crane)

14″ "Margot Ballerina". #1535-1957 and tagged: Madame Alexander. White tutu with red rose, flowers in hair and ballerina slippers. (Courtesy Sandra Crane)

16″ "Margot Ballerina". #1635-1957. All original. Hard plastic with vinyl oversleeved arms, jointed elbows and ankles. (Courtesy Florence Black Musich)

14″ "Marine". All composition and original. (Wendy). Marks: Alexander, on head. Tag: Marine/Madame Alexander/New York/All Rights Reserved. (Courtesy Pat Sebastian)

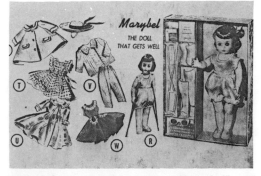

FAO Schwarz catalog carried "Marybel" and clothes for her. Top to bottom: White pique coat and straw hat, checkered dress, satin robe, striped cotton pajamas and red cotton play dress. 1959.

These outfits were sold in the 1959 FAO Schwarz catalog for Kelly, Marybel and Edith the Lonely doll. (E) Coral coat and hat; (F) Nylon robe; (G) Pink crepe nightie; (H) Party dress; (J) Petticoat and panties; (K) Called a sport dress. These outfits came in both 16″ and 22″ sizes.

1960 FAO Schwarz catalog shows these clothes for either the Mary-Bel or Polly: (D) Lace and embroidery trimmed nightie; (E) Pink satin robe; (F) Playsuit and skirt; (G) Nylon print dress and (H) Rose velvet coat.

#1575 16″ "Marybel" of 1960. Came in this trousseau case with dress, petticoat, panties, satin housecoat, slippers and socks. Catalog reprint.

This Marybel doll is unusual and rare. #1570-1965. She has long, very straight hair with full bangs. Catalog reprint.

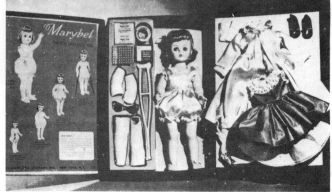

31″ "Mary Ellen" in a red coat of heavy pile fleece with brass buttons. Taffeta dress. Hat and muff of leopard plush. #3133. Catalog reprint.

31″ "Mary Ellen" of 1954. Walker, head turns. Plastic and vinyl and with rooted hair. Nylon net lace over taffeta gown. Pink sash and slippers. Circlet of flowers in hair. Catalog reprint. #3135.

31″ "Mary Ellen" in bridesmaid gown of yellow taffeta trimmed with gold braid, appliqued flowers (bodice) and rhinestones. Bandeau hat of taffeta with tiny flower clusters at each ear and a gold mesh veil. #3160. Catalog reprint.

This 1955 "Mary Ellen" sold for $32.95 from the FAO Schwarz catalog and is dressed in a rose-pink organdy dress, trimmed with lace. Straw bonnet is tied with large bow.

31″ "Mary Ellen" of 1955 is shown in a period gown of aqua-blue taffeta. Bonnet and muff are of matching tulle trimmed with rosebuds. #3162. Catalog reprint.

This 31″ "Mary Ellen" was in the 1955 FAO Schwarz catalog for $29.95. The dress is red taffeta redingote over a red dotted white frock which could be worn by itself. Straw hat is white, black suede slippers and white socks. This dress matches the 1955 Cissy-faced "Binnie" #1518-15″, #1818-18″ and #2518-25″.

This 31″ "Mary Ellen" sold in FAO Schwarz catalog in 1955 for $49.95. Hard plastic and vinyl. Jointed knees. This gown is mauve taffeta with bodice and overskirt of matching shadow check taffeta. Overskirt is caught up with flowers. Pink satin slippers and large straw poke bonnet with bow. This dress was not described as an "exclusive", nor shown in Alexander catalog.

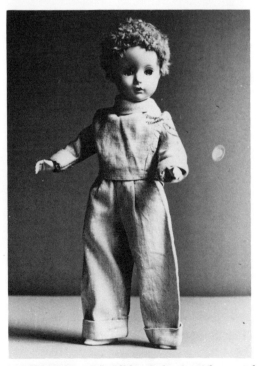

14″ "Mary Mine". #3350-1977. Cloth body with vinyl head and limbs. Sleep blue eyes and rooted hair. Original. (Courtesy Renie Culp)

14″ "Mary Martin". All hard plastic with caracul wig. Original blue "jumpsuit" with name embroidered in red. Tagged South Pacific. 1950. (Margaret). (Courtesy Roberta Jackson)

9″ "McGuffey Ana". All composition with eyes painted to side. Tag: McGuffey Ana Madame Alexander N.Y. U.S.A. The two on the left are courtesy of Lesley Richards and one on right is courtesy of Barbara Boury.

9″ "McGuffey Ana" of 1935-1939. All composition with painted eyes to side. (Courtesy Roberta Lago)

11¼″ Rare size "McGuffey Ana". All composition. Red/White check dress with rick-rack trim and white pinafore with lace trim. Hat is missing and shoes have been replaced. Marked Princess Elizabeth on head and dress tagged McGuffey Ana. 1938. (Courtesy Susan Goetz)

13″ "McGuffey Ana". All composition with brown sleep eyes. Tag: Madame Alexander/New York USA. Head is marked with a ⊗ circle X and she has "13", on back. (Courtesy Lesley Richards)

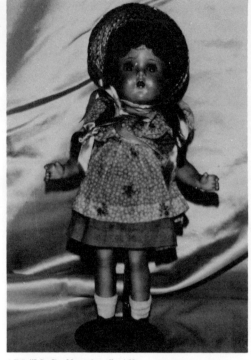

15″ "McGuffey Ana". All composition with sleep eyes and open mouth. All original and in her original box. Head is marked Princess Elizabeth and tag: McGuffey Ana. 1937. Blue dress. (Courtesy Marge Meisinger)

13″ "McGuffey Ana". (Princess Elizabeth). All original and hair in original style. Bent right arm, painted lower lashes, brown sleep eyes and eye shadow. (Courtesy Dianne Hoffman)

14″ "McGuffey Ana" as shown in the 1941 National Porges Corp. (Chicago) catalog. The suitcase is 20″ with a wood frame. Doll has open mouth, human hair wig and is dressed in organdy. Included are dimity dress, embroidered pinafore, pocketbook, embroidered hankie, extra shoes, socks, nightie and spun rayon coat and hat to match. Case, clothes and doll sold for $4.56.

13″ "McGuffey Ana" came in this trousseau case in 1940. The case is 20″ and a wood frame. Catalog reprint.

This "McGuffey Ana" doll of 1956 came in 18", 25" and 31" sizes with prices of $15.95, $22.95 and $34.75. Ad says she is dressed in lace trimmed dotted swiss dress with feather stitched white organdy pinafore over a hoop petticoat, straw hat, pocketbook, white socks and high button shoes. Hard plastic with vinyl over-sleeved arms.

16" "Melinda" in blue organdy and lace. #1620-1963. Jointed waist. Also came in 14" and 22" size in this dress. Marks: Alexander/ 1963, on head. Tag: Melinda. (Courtesy Linda Crowsey)

Dining Room set 1957 from FAO Schwarz is five pieces finished in blonde maple. Table has two drop leaves and is 8¾" by 6¾" when open. Sold for $12.00. Catalog reprint.

20" "Melinda", as sold through Marshall Field. Rigid vinyl body with jointed waist. Vinyl head with very long rooted hair. (Kelly). Blue sleep eyes. Blue organdy gown with many rows of ruffles. Came in red/white tin trunk with extra tagged Madame Alexander clothes. Marks: Alexander, on head. Tag: Melinda by Madame Alexander, etc. 1963. (Courtesy Sharon Ivy)

Nursery set is from 1957. Sold through FAO Schwarz.
Five piece set of wood scaled for 8″ dolls (baby). Finished
in pink with blue trim. The wardrobe is 10½″ high. Set
sold for $8.95. Catalog reprint.

Stylish five piece dining room set offered by FAO Schwarz
in 1958 to fit Alexander dolls. Hutch is 8½″ high. Table
top is 7½″ long and 4″ high. Set sold for $8.95. Catalog
reprint.

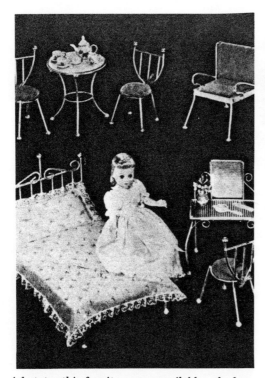

Ad states this furniture was available only from
the Alexander Doll Company. 1957.

Bedroom set is from FAO Schwarz in 1957. The four poster bed is
12″ long, finished in blonde maple. Skirted vanity and bench. Sold
for $6.95. Catalog reprint.

Wardrobe is 13½″ high and 9″ wide and 5″ deep, with mahogany finish. (Sold for $6.95). The colonial bed is 15¾″ long, 9½″ wide and 14¾″ high. The spread, canopy, bolster and mattress is dotted swiss covered. Mahogany finish and sold for $8.00. The matching clothes rack is 4″ by 9½″ by 10½″. Full length drawer on the bottom and is also mahogany finished. Sold for $3.00. All from FAO Schwarz in 1958. Catalog reprint.

Five piece living room set from 1958 (FAO Schwarz). Maple finish and blue corduroy upholstery. Divan is 11″ long and 6½″ high. The set sold for $8.00. Catalog reprint.

1 BEDROOM SET ....
e set featuring an 11″ four-poster bed

FAO Schwarz shows an unidentified Wendy/ Alexander-kin with this furniture. She is of the Little Madaline type. The bedroom set cost $13.95 and the doll $6.95. 1964.

Listed on box (Alexander) is Style #30. The contents were six sets of spread and pillow (foam filled) for "Little Genius". They came with pink or blue roses, and tied with a ribbon.

42″ tall display stand from the Madame Alexander Co. On heavy wire stand that allows it to rotate. Plastic bubbles hold the dolls. It is a four-sided stand. Date is unknown. It is known that this same idea, only made flat like a picture frame, with the bubbles, was used during the early 1950's. (Courtesy Martha Gragg)

Pink clothes rack made of wood is shown in its original box. Box says Style #49. (Courtesy Jay Minter)

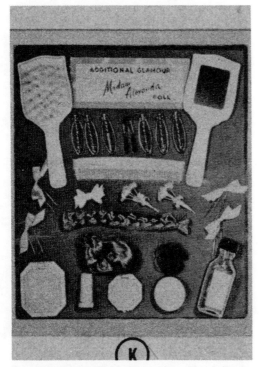

Boxed items for all Madame Alexander dolls that include curlers, hair pieces, ribbons, mirror and brush. Sold through FAO Schwarz catalogs. 1951.

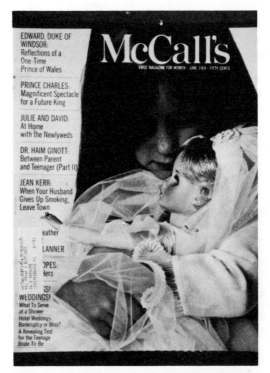

The June 1969 cover of McCall's Magazine featured this bride doll. (Madame Alexander's "Elise")

7½″ Wendy dressed as "Little Victoria" #376-1953. Mint and original. (Courtesy LaDonna Dolan)

8″ "Southern Belle" of 1956. There were two this year and the other outfit is shown in a catalog reprint in the black and white section. (Courtesy Jay Minter)

8″ "Baby Clown" #464-1955. With his dog Huggy, and bright red caracul wig, he is a delightful little fellow. The outfit is half pale blue and half "hot" pink. Gold boots. Tag: Alexander-kins Madame Alexander. (Courtesy Bernice Heister)

7½″ Wendy-Kins baby. 1954. One-piece stuffed and posable vinyl body and limbs. Hard plastic heads. One has molded hair and other has caracul wig. Both are open mouth/nurser. Both came in plain white boxes marked Dayton's G. Dept. (sidewards) 660/$1.98. The molded hair doll wears a plastic lined, cotton lace diaper, the other has matching unlined panties and bonnet. Both have pink socks tied with pink ribbon. Both have tags that are pink letters on white: Wendy-Kin/Madame Alexander/Reg. U.S. Pat. Off N.Y. U.S.A. (Courtesy Pat Gardner)

7½" "Wendy" #375-1953 called "Country Picnic". Cotton gown, pique white jacket, straw hat with flowers. Straight-leg non-walker. Tag: Alexander-kin. (Courtesy Bernice Heister)

8" Alexander-kin as "Lissy". From the Americana Series #487-1961. This one is tagged: "Lissy"/Madame Alexander etc. and is dressed in one piece pink organdy/ lace trim blouse and pink, lace trim full length slip. Jumper dress is black polished cotton with lavender flowers. Bend knee walker.

8" "Story Princess" #892-1956. Rose nylon tulle with rose underslip lined in white. White pantaloons. Wand and tiara are replaced. Bend-knee walker. Matches the larger Cissy-faced "Story Princess" that came in a 15" and 18" size. From the N.B.C. Television show, "Howdy-Doody." (Courtesy Bernice Heister)

8" Alexander-kin as "Southern Belle" #385-1964. Matches the 1963 Lissy Southern Belle Classic.

8″ "Wendy" #392-1957. Bright blue cotton shirt with white top and suspender Tyrolean outfit. White felt peaked hat. Original except replaced shoes. Tag: Alexander-kin Madame Alexander. Bend-knee walker. (Courtesy Bernice Heister)

8″ School dress #460-1954. Tag: Alexander-kin. Straight-leg walker. This outfit was made in 1953 on a straight-leg non-walker with blue dress and roll brim hat and in 1954 with this yellow dress and wide brim hat. The 1955 one had a chartreuse dress and small brim hat with flowers. (Courtesy Linda Crowsey)

8″ "Hansel" #445-1955. Straight-leg non-walker. White felt cap, black velvet trousers, white shirt and striped stockings. Shorter cut hair-do. Tagged: Alexander-kin. (Courtesy Dave and Kathy Ethington)

8″ "Wendy Walker" tagged Alexander-kins. #458-1955. Has straight legs. Wears white organdy pinafore over pink organdy dress and straw hat with flowers. All original. (Courtesy Pat Spirek)

26″ "Baby Genius." All one-piece, stuffed laytex body and limbs. Hard plastic head. Mohair wig over molded hair. All original. 1949. (Courtesy Barbara Boury)

8″ "Going To Grandma's". Bend-knee walker and tagged: Alexander-kin. #566-1956. (Courtesy Linda Crowsey)

18″ "Arlene Dahl." 1950. (Maggie with heavy painted features). Inspired by musical biography "Three Little Words" about songwriters Bert Kalmar and Harry Ruby. (Played by Fred Astair and Red Skelton). The red-head, Arlene Dahl, played Eileen Percy, who married Ruby. Vera Ellen and Gloria DeHaven were also in this happy and fun-filled movie. This same doll/gown, as a blonde, was used for the 1951 Portrait Group. All hard plastic with flat feet. Doll not marked. Tag: Madame Alexander/All Rights Reserved/ New York U.S.A. Also wears Fashion Academy Award tag on wrist. Dress in lavender taffeta with sheer over skirt with flowers and rhinestones, pearl necklace and rhinestone earrings. Pink taffeta slip, silk stockings and lavender shoes. (Courtesy Dave and Kathy Ethington)

14″ "Aunt Pitty Pat" from the movie "Gone With The Wind." All composition (Wendy), painted lashes and eye shadow. Very light red mohair wig. Sleep blue eyes. All original. Gown designed from scene of Melanie's party. See black and white section for costume still from the movie. 1939. (Courtesy Dianne Hoffman)

Side view of "Aunt Pitty Pat's" beautiful bonnet. The actual one in the movie had much more lace around the face. (Courtesy Dianne Hoffman)

This is the back view of the bonnet as worn by "Aunt Pitty Pat" in the "Gone With The Wind" movie. (Courtesy Dianne Hoffman)

8″ "Bible Character." The owner calls her "Sarah", but her real name is not known for certain. The tie around the body is wrapped twice, and she has four punch-through metal brads on the trim of the bodice. These same brads are on the head piece (red ones) and hold the chiffon scarf back. Tag: Alexander-kin/by Madame Alexander/Reg. U.S. Pat. Off. N.Y., N.Y. (Courtesy Marianne's Doll House, Billie McCabe)

"Bride and Honeymoon Trousseau" is shown in the Alexander catalog "Album of Dolls". 1941-1942, although a couple of items of clothes are missing. (Wendy). (Courtesy Marge Meisinger)

18" "Bride". Composition marked Alexander on head and dress label: Princess Elizabeth. (Margaret) Goes with 21" "Groom" from the Royal Wedding set of 1947. The specially designed half slip accentuates the line of the ribbed faile wedding gown. Flowers hold the net floor length veil and matches bouquet tied to wrist. (Courtesy Elizabeth Montesano, Yesterday's Children)

13" "Betty". 1935. All composition with bent right arms. Blonde mohair wig covers Patsy-type molded hairstyle. Yellow organdy dress is trimmed with ruffles, yellow ribbons and a pink rosette. (Courtesy Rose Montesano)

20″ "Cissy Walking Her Dog". #2025-1956 and made for the Abraham & Strauss stores. (Courtesy Shirley's Dollhouse, Wheeling, Ill.)

14″ "Cinderella, Poor", #1536-1952. (Margaret). All hard plastic. All cotton dress has grey skirt with red check patch, grey sleeves, brown bodice with black rick-rack and yellow cross stitches. White apron attached and pulled up at the side and stitched. White head scarf. Marked with a very light. Alex. on head. Tag: Madame Alexander/New York/All Rights Reserved. (Courtesy Mary Partridge)

"Cissette" is shown in display box of 1963. Dressed in extra Cissette outfit. This packaging came with two extra wigs, held on with velcro strips. (Courtesy Sherry Kraft)

Yachting outfits: "Cissy" #2205-1958, "Elise" #1720-1958 and "Cissette" #808-1958. All have red or navy blue pipping on legs of slacks. Wore either red or navy blue high heel sandals. (All courtesy Charmaine Shields)

10½″ "Cissette in Dancing Gown" #830-1961. Elaborate hairdo. This is a beautiful, very mint doll. (Courtesy Roberta Lago)

7″ Composition named: "Colonial". White mohair wig with black bow and carries black lace handkerchief. (Tiny Betty)(Courtesy Sandra Crane)

14″ "Dr. Defoe" and 13″ "Nurse" (Betty). Dr. has painted blue eyes with painted upper lashes only. Smiling face, dimple in chin, grey mohair wig over molded hair. Right arm slightly bent, dressed in original three-piece outfit of one-piece jump suit, top shirt that ties in back and long doctor's coat. Doll is unmarked. Tag: Madame Alexander New York. Black patent leather shoes with buckle. Nurse has red mohair wig. Dressed in white short legged jump suit type pants, then two layer skirt and slip, also cap and a bent right arm and dimples. (Courtesy Dianne Hoffman)

16″ "Elise Ballerina." #1740-1962. Green eyes and a wax-like look to the hard plastic. Vinyl over-sleeved arms and jointed at elbows, knees and ankles. (Courtesy Lilah Beck)

21″ "Gainsbourough Cissy" #2176-1975. One of the "Cissy Models Her Formal Gowns" series. All taffeta with flowers on the sleeves and hat. The hat is natural straw. (Courtesy Marge Meisinger)

18″ "Goldilocks". Made especially for the Dallas Nieman-Markus store. 1951. Blonde "flock" wig with two rows of hanging curls in back and upper hair tied with black ribbon. (Maggie) Blue sleep eyes. Blue dress with vest look in front, showing white "blouse". Tag: Madame Alexander/All Rights Reserved. Dress was also sold separately for 18″ size #217-1951-52. Belt is missing (black). (Courtesy Sharon Ivy)

14″ "John Powers Model". 1952. All hard plastic with brown sleep eyes and blonde saran wig. (Maggie). Marks on box: Power's Model number 1521T and on black hat box: Madame Alexander Presents the John Robert Powers Model. This hat box contains comb and six pink rollers. Tag: John Powers Model/Madame Alexander New York. U.S.A. This particular doll was given by the C.H. Mastin Carpet Co. to it's top salesman, and helped introduced Saran carpeting. 1952 and 1953. Given to the owner's father when he was distributor for Mastin Co. (Courtesy Sandy Fleckenstein)

20″ "Kathryn Grayson." All hard plastic (Margaret). Heavy make-up and fuller lips with false eyelashes over regular ones. Tag: Madame Alexander, etc. Inspired from the movie "Midnight Kiss", which was Mario Lanza's first film. Madame Alexander has always tried to promote "the better things in life", to children through her dolls, and good music and singers were not ignored. Lanza, after this film, had critics saying he was a new Caruso. "Midnight Kiss" was a Joe Pasternak musical and also starred Jose Iturbi, Ethel Barrymore and Keenan Wynn. Directed by Norman Taurog. 1949. It was quickly followed in 1950, by another Pasternak-Taurog film, "The Toast To New Orleans", in which the song, "Be My Love" made such a hit. This film also included David Nivan and Rita Moreno. (Courtesy Sherry Kraft)

18″ "Karen Ballerina". Karen Booth was the Prima Ballerina who co-starred with Margaret O'Brien in the movie, "The Unfinished Dance". All composition with flock-type hair in braids, blue sleep eyes and all original. Doll is marked: Mme. Alexander on head and Alexander on back. (Margaret). Came with pink or blue roses in hair. 1946. (Courtesy Sandy Fleckenstein)

21″ "Jackie" and wardrobe designed exclusively for the Marshall Field stores in 1962. The trunk is vinyl over plywood -24″ X 12½″ and has plastic binding. This outfit sold for $65.00 in 1962.

15″ "Pierre" and "Zaza" Poodles. "Fur" with looped yarn longer fur, felt heart shaped noses and felt over the eyes, which are plastic. Inset lashes. Both are original. Tag pasted on underside of each. (Courtesy Shirley's Doll House, Wheeling, Ill)

The Marshall Field catalog in 1966 showed this 21″ Jacqueline doll as "Margot" in a 24″ Louis Vuitton trunk with wardrobe. This ensemble sold for $250.00 in 1966. Included was a mink stole and hat.

11″ (sitting) "Suzzette" of 1954. Poodle is black and pink. Plastic eyes and collar with rhinestones. (Courtesy Margaret Mandel)

This doll is an Alexander-Cissy and is dressed in the outfit for the "Circus on Ice" #1962-1963.

This number was called "Circus on Ice" and was performed in the 22nd Edition of the Ice Capades during the 1962-1963 season.

This is the grand finale called "Strike Up the Band" in the 1968 Ice Capades program.

21″ "Strike Up the Band". 27th Edition. 1968.
(Jacqueline).

Side view of "Strike Up the Band".

This 24″ Kaysam doll is dressed from the 1971-1972 number "World of Nostalgia".

24″ From the 29th Edition of Ice Capades of 1970 and the number called "Indian Splendor", this doll is dressed as one of the "Bird Maidens" from that number. The doll is marked Kaysam.

24″ "Legend of Frozen Time" from the 31st Edition of Ice Capades of 1971-1972. Marks: Kaysam. 1961.

This is a photo shown in the 1972 Ice Capades program and shows the Ice Capets dressed in the "The Legend Of Frozen Time".

20″ Alexander Jacqueline doll was used for 1961-1962 "My Fair Lady".

21" Alexander Jacqueline doll used for 1966-1967 "The King Lives On". Fantastic hair-do with three large curls, feathers and tiara.

21" "Judy" from the film "Meet Me In St. Louis" composition (Wendy). The movie gown that inspired this gown can be seen on the cover of "Meet Me In St. Louis" sheet music. This gown is the same design as the doll shown in Marjorie Uhl's and Jan Foulke's books, but the material, color and treatment of the hem and collars are different. (Courtesy Beth French. Photo by Dr. Deanne Bell)

This 24" marked Kaysam 1961 doll was used for the costume of the finale to the 30th Edition of the Ice Capades in 1970 and called "The American Girl".

24" Called "Baby Doll Precision", this Ice Capades doll is from the 30th Edition in 1970-1971. The doll is marked Kaysam/ 1961. The number this doll was used in was called "Welcome to Our World", and the main performers were Kathy and Jamie Beard, along with the Ice Capets.

20″ "My Fair Lady". 22nd Edition 1962-1963. (Cissy).

14″ "Beth" of Little Women. 1950. Blue dress with pink roses. (Courtesy Dianne Hoffman)

This is the back of the head of "Beth". (Courtesy Dianne Hoffman)

14″ "Jo" from the 1950 set of Little Women. Green dress with yellow rick-rack and ribbon. (Maggie)(Courtesy of Dianne Hoffman)

This is the back of the "Jo" hairdo. (Courtesy Dianne Hoffman)

14″ "Meg" in pale blue with inset organdy bodice and pink ribbons. 1950. (Courtesy Dianne Hoffman)

The back of "Meg's" head. (Courtesy Dianne Hoffman)

14″ "Amy" of Little Women. She has the loop curls that are usually on the "Jo" doll, and this set may have been mis-tagged at the factory. (Courtesy Dianne Hoffman)

This photo shows the back of the "Amy" head and the loop curls used in the early years of hard plastic. (Courtesy Dianne Hoffman)

14" "Marme" from the 1950 set of Little Women. (Courtesy Dianne Hoffman)

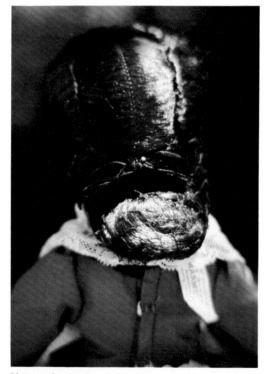

Shows the back of the head and hairdo of the 1950 "Marme".

14" "Beth" showing the bending knees. (Courtesy Mary Partridge)

14″ "Amy" from the 1955 set of Little Women. She is all original and shows the variation of material used. The polka dots are larger on this gown. (Courtesy Marian Schmuhl)

This is the 14″ "Amy" of the 1955 set of Little Women. She is all original, does not have the bending knees, but does have the large hands the rest of the set has. (Courtesy Mary Partridge)

This shows the 1955 set of Little Women together. All but "Amy" have bending knees. All have the large, wide-spread hands, and were from the same year as the Binnie Walker that was so successful. (Courtesy Mary Partridge)

14″ "Jo" of the 1955 set of Little Women. All hard plastic with bending knees. All original. (Courtesy Mary Partridge)

14″ "Meg" of the 1955 set of Little Women. All hard plastic with bending knees. All original. (Courtesy Mary Partridge)

14″ "Beth". Hard plastic and all original. Bend knees and large hands. From 1955 set of Little Women. (Courtesy Mary Partridge)

Margaret-faced "Marme" #1500 of the 1955 set that shows the variation of the color and print. (Courtesy Sandra Crane)

"Marme" is 14″, all hard plastic with bending knees from the 1955 set of Little Women. See this set as offered in the FAO Schwarz catalog of 1955 in the black and white section. Variations of prints were used. (Courtesy Mary Partridge)

This "Marme" is from the 1955 and 1956 set of Little Women and shows a variation of the print used. All original. (Courtesy Mary Partridge)

8″ Little Women set used in 1953 and 1954. Note the early Alexander-kins tags. (Courtesy Ethel Stewart. Photo by Ted Long)

23½" "Lilibet". All composition, open mouth, sleep eyes. (Princess Elizabeth). Head marked: Madame Alexander/Princess Elizabeth. Original dress with tag: "Lilibet" Madame Alexander, etc. "Lilibet" became the pet name for Elizabeth (Princess) originated by herself, who as a child, could not pronounce her own name, Elizabeth. The following quotes are from the books: "The Little Princess" by Marion Crawford, Harcourt, Brace and Company/1950 . . page 16 . . "From the time of my arrival, Lilibet came down to me. She had given herself the name when she found "Elizabeth" rather difficult to get around, and it had stuck to her ever since."

From "Majesty" by Robert Lacey, copyright 1977 Avon Books. "He (George V-grandfather) called her "Lilibet" for as she learned to talk and attempted her own name she could only lisp "Lilliebeth". The name stuck. She was Lilibet to her family from then onwards". This doll's hairstyle and shoes are also original. (Courtesy Beth French. Photo by Dr. Deanne Bell)

14" "Margot Ballerina". #1550-1954. Hard plastic. (Margaret). Pink tutu with rhinestones on bodice. Also came in blue. (Courtesy Sherry Kraft)

18" "Margot Ballerina" in red. All original and tagged. (Maggie). All hard plastic. 1951.

13″ Marked "Circle X", composition skater in red plaid ribbed corduroy, matching mitts and cap. Panties are separate. (Runners are missing from skates). Open mouth/teeth, blue tin sleep eyes/lashes and mohair wig, with bangs and braids. Also marked 13 on back. Sold from Wards, late-1930's. (Courtesy Elizabeth Montesano, Yesterday's Children)

9″ "McGuffey Ana". All composition and all original. (Wendy Ann). (Courtesy Barbara Boury)

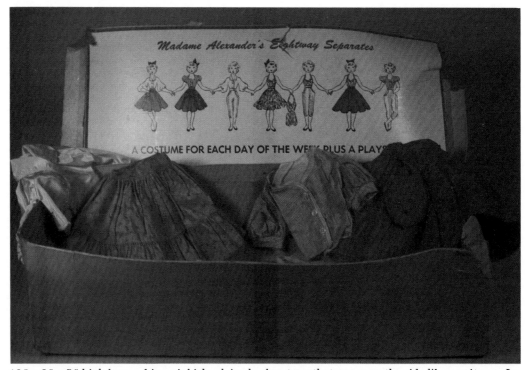

19″ x 8″ x 5″ high box and is a pinkish, plain shoebox type that opens on the side like a suitcase. Inside cover is red and white and reads: Madame Alexander's Eightway Separates . . . then shows seven Maggie-type dolls in the various ways the outfits can be mixed and matched. A costume for each day of the week. Some of the clothing is still with the box and tagged: Madame Alexander/All Rights Reserved /New York U.S.A. (Courtesy Sandra Crane)

12″ 1962 #1290 "Pamela" (Lissy). All hard plastic. Shown in original box. Some of the clothing is missing. (Courtesy Marge Meisinger)

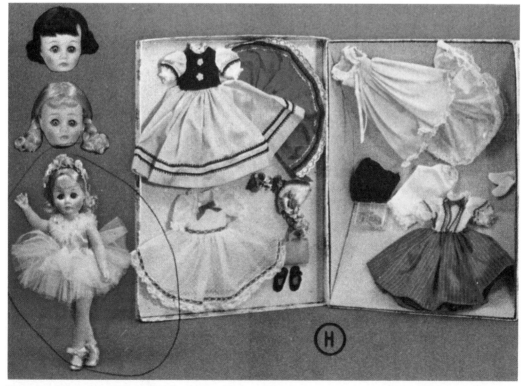

The 1970 "Pamela and Party Kit" sold for $29.95. This was an exclusive with FAO Schwarz. The 12″ doll is in an 18″ case and clothes included ballet, peasant apron, nightie, dotted swiss party dress and a blonde and brunette wig.

12″ "Pamela and Party Kit" was an exclusive for FAO Schwarz in 1971. The case is 18″ and doll was dressed in ballerina outfit and additional costumes included a peasant apron, a nightie, taffeta party dress and accessories. A blonde and brunette wig was also included. This item cost $34.95 in 1971.

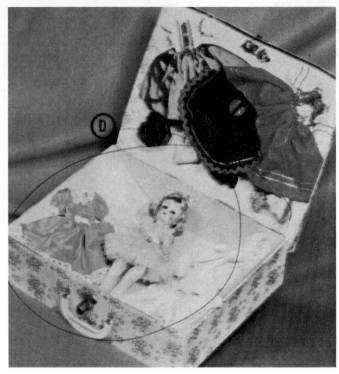

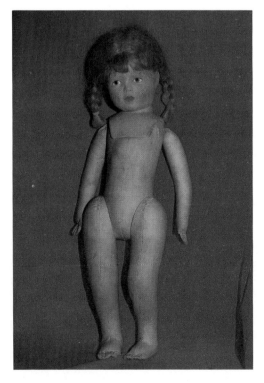

20″ undressed but original wig. Hard plastic shoulder plate head with flesh tone flocking on it, painted features, and hard stuffed cloth body. Stitched fingers, jointed legs and stitched toes. She is marked: Mme Alexander, on back of the head in raised letters. Ca. 1950's. The doll resembles the Kathe Kruse dolls. It has been examined by more than one collector and there is no question that it is a marked Alexander doll. (Courtesy Maxine Look)

8″ "Ringbearer" to the Wedding Party-1950. Wears white satin suit made in one piece made to look like two pieces. White leather oxfords with two eyelets. Lace at collar, sleeve and down front. Golden blonde hair, blue eyes with dark molded lashes and painted lashes below eyes. Carries white satin pillow tied with white ribbon. Rhinestone ring in middle of pillow. Gold tag on left wrist: Madame Alexander, on one side. Other: Madame Alexander Made of finest plastic. Can be washed. Cloth tag at neck: Madame Alexander N.Y. Box: Style 10-Ringbear. He is also wearing a cotton jersey vest and cotton muslin boxer shorts. (Lovey-Dovey). (Courtesy Ethel Stewart)

12″ "Rozy" #1130-1969. This doll was made as Rozy for one year only. (Courtesy Renie Culp)

7″ "Rumbero and Rumbera of Cuba." (Tiny Betty). All brown painted composition with painted eyes to the side. All original. Black mohair wigs. (Courtesy Marge Meisinger)

Royal Group with 17″ hard plastic: "Queen Elizabeth"-1954, 14″ "Princess Margaret Rose"-1953, 8″ "Prince Charles" and 8″ "Princess Anne"-1957. (Courtesy Sherry Kraft)

21″ "Sonja Henie". Composition and all original, only missing her skates. Hair in original set. This Christmas outfit is one of the rarest. Cap is green with white "fur" trim, as are the gloves. The gloves are attached to each other with a string. (Courtesy Dianne Hoffman)

22″ "Sonja Henie" that is mint and original. Brown sleep eyes and dimples. All composition. (Courtesy Dianne Hoffman)

15″ "Sonja Henie". Composition with gold skates, pink rosebuds in human hair wig and simple rayon satin dress is marked "Ballerina". Dress length white rabbit cape came with the doll. Marked Sonja Henie/ Madame Alexander, on head. (Courtesy Elizabeth Montesano, Yesterday's Children)

This is a beautiful photo of the 22″ "Sonja Henie" doll. (Courtesy Dianne Hoffman)

This is the front of the wrist booklet that came with the Lissy "Brigitta" of the "Sound of Music" set dressed in sailor suits. It shows a complete set of "Sound of Music" dolls using the 8″ Alexander-kins dolls. It is not known if this set was marketed or not. Booklet courtesy Loramay Wilson.

It is not known if the very first set was completely made up in sailor suits to sell, or not. There seems to be several "Brigitta" dolls around, but the others have not shown up. It is also possible that the sailor suits were packaged separately. This photo is from the wrist booklet and shows Lissy, Janie, Smarty and Mary Ann.

The children await inspection before studies begin. Kurt, tired of waiting, sat down.

7″ "Tiny Bettys". All composition with painted eyes to the side. Red/blue trimmed white rayon taffeta gown is called "American Girl". She has a cotton flag attached to wrist. Other is called "Birthday Doll"/November. She wears a plain navy velvet dress with matching cap tied with pink ribbons. (Courtesy Elizabeth Montesano, Yesterday's Children)

158

14″ "Wendy Bride". Hard plastic. Box marked #1552. Doll not marked. Tag: Madame Alexander/All Rights Reserved. Carries hat box and has gold medal for costume excellence. "Flowergirl" is hard plastic and unmarked. Tag: Madame Alexander, etc. Has hat box. Flowers in hair. Both dolls are walkers. Box #1535 for Flowergirl. (Courtesy Barbra Jean Male. Photo by Michael Male)

13″ "Wendy Ann" in riding habit. All composition with swivel waist and marked on the body Wendy Ann/Mme Alexander New York. Right arm bent, blue sleep eyes, eye shadow and painted lower lashes. Red vest with brass buttons and black neck tie. (Courtesy Dianne Hoffman)

1968 14″ #1495 "Scarlett" made this one year only. The Alexander catalog shows this doll in a different print gown. (Mary Ann.)

The Nancy Ann Doll Co.'s "Queen" was shown on page 103 and is shown again in the black and white section of this book. She is also shown here in a comparision study between two Madame Alexander dolls. The descriptions are as follows: (Marks on "Queen"-with crown-crest is where buttons are glued on to give her a chest.) The blue eyed doll is marked Alexander (Margaret), is a flat-footed ballerina with a walker mechanism. She is 17", bust 9" circ., waist is 7" circ, hips 9" circ. Fingernails are un-painted and all fingers are separated. The other outside doll is also an Alexander, is flat footed, but a non-walker and is also a ballerina, but in a different costume. Her measurements are the same as the other Alexander, but her fingernails are painted a very pale pearlized pink shade. The Nancy Ann "Queen" (crown) measurements are approx. as above on the Alexanders, but seem to be about ½" smaller at bust and hips. These are hard to measure because of the arm and leg joints. (Courtesy Elizabeth Montesano, Yesterday's Children)

The hands of the brown-eyed Alexander and Nancy Ann are similar, but they have different finishes on them. All wrists measure 2" circ.

18" Nancy Ann doll of 1952. All hard plastic and original. Neither doll nor clothes are tagged. Courtesy Roberta Lago.

This is the back of the small gold-colored medal that came with most Alexander dolls in 1952 and 1953.

Shows the front of the metal medallion that came on most Alexander dolls in 1952 and 1953. The Alexander Doll Company and Madame Alexander were awarded the Gold Medal for Fashion in 1951, 1952 and 1953.

Simplicity Printed Patterns #1809. Ca. 1956-1958. These patterns could be used for Alexander-kin's, Ginny and Muffie dolls and are very much like the style used by Alexander Doll Co.

21″ "Victoria" 1945-1946. (Princess Flavia of 1939.) All composition. Shown from a Frost Bros. ad. (Courtesy of Fannie Nedbalek)

21″ "Melaine" in same Frost Bros. ad of 1945. Caption is shown in other picture. (Courtesy Fannie Nedbalek.)

21″ "Antoinette" with platinum curls and a full Marie Antoinette gown of pink fille, trimmed with star sequins, rosebuds and lace. Jewels in hair, on wrists and fingers. (Courtesy Fannie Nedbalek.)

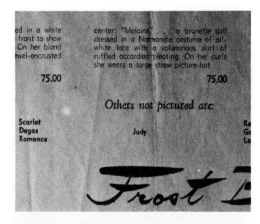

Frost Bros. ad listing other Portraits available in 1945-1946. Renoir, Godey, Lady Windermere. (Courtesy Fannie Nedbalek.)

These dolls were shown in the 1951 FAO Schwarz catalog. (D) "Sunflower" the clown with pom-pom nose and flower eyes, dressed in satin, neck ruff and felt hat. 40″ tall and cost $12.95.(C) "Frou-Frou." Dressed in soft green ballerina over a ruffled net petticoat, pink ballet slippers and lilac colored yarn hair. 40″ and cost $18.00. (B) "Clarabelle" came in sizes 19″, 29″ and 40″. (A) "Girl On The Flying Trapeze." Dressed in bouffant pink satin and satin slippers. 40″ tall, she cost $18.00.

"Mary Muslin" with pansy eyes, yarn hair. All cloth. Came in sizes 19″, 26″ and 40″ and was in the 1951 FAO Schwarz catalog. The uke and trunk were not included in her price. ($5.95, $10.00 and $15.95.)

8″ Alexander-kin made into an "Infant of Prague". It is not known if the arms were positioned at the factory. There is no question that the crown was made by the Alexander Company, and the materials are exactly the same as used on the 1950's ballerinas, queens and others. The backing is lucent-plastic and the overlay is the "tin" type gold with rhinestones and pearls. This doll is not listed in any of the Alexander Company catalogs. (Courtesy Peggy Lewis.)

These arms did not come out of a mold, but were formed in a very professional manner, such as by the use of hot sand, or with heat in some way that did not damage the arm.

14″ "Mommie and Me". See the following photo for the ad on this doll of 1954. All hard plastic. (Margaret). Her hat had a veil and she most likely had a belt. Navy blue taffeta with white collar and cuffs. Walker, head turns and has large hands with wide spread fingers. Tag: Madame Alexander/Mommie and Me. (Courtesy Helena Street.)

14″ "Mommie and Me" ad from the December 1954 Better Homes and Gardens Magazine. It isn't possible to tell much about the "baby", but it may have been a molded hair Wendy-kin of 1954. (Courtesy Marge Meisinger)

20″ "Mommie's Pet". #7135-1976. Vinyl head and limbs with a cloth body. Sleep eyes and rooted hair. Marks: Alexander/1973. Still Available. (Courtesy Renie Culp.)

21″ "Mommie's Pet". #7130-1978. Cloth and vinyl with rooted auburn hair, blue sleep eyes. Pink cotton dress with white eyelet apron. Pink cotton sun bonnet with eyelet trim on brim. Marks: Alexander 1978/6. Tag: Mommie's Pet. (Courtesy Kathleen Rudisill.)

14″ "Miss America". All composition with blonde mohair wig, closed mouth and sleep eyes. Right hand molded in fist to hold flag. Marks: MME Alexander, on head. Tag: Miss America/ Madame Alexander NY USA/All Rights Reserved. Wears original red/white striped pique dress. (Wendy Ann). Made for 1939 World's Fair held in New York. Also one rode along with the Freedom Train sent across the U.S. in 1940. (Courtesy Glorya Woods.)

7½″ "Normandy", shown with her original flowered box. All composition with side painted eyes and painted on shoes and socks. (Tiny Betty). Tag: Normandy, Mme. Alexander, etc. 1935-38. (Courtesy Nancy Roeder.)

7½″ "Nurse". All composition and original. (Tiny Betty). Shoes are painted on and white. Bent right arm and eyes painted to the side. (Courtesy Marge Meisinger.)

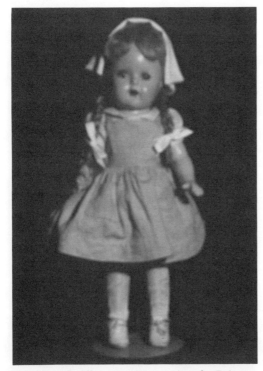

15″ "Nurse". All composition, using the Princess Elizabeth mold, and so marked. Heavy blue cotton with white blouse, long white stockings with white oxford shoes. Cap is a replacement. Blouse is tagged: Nurse/Madame Alexander All Rights Reserved. (Courtesy Bernice Heister.)

20″ "Old Fashioned Girl", from Louisa May Alcott book of the same name. All hard plastic (Margaret). Has human hair blonde wig in curls at nape of neck and two curls that hang down. Hairdo is tied with ribbon. Gown is white and has hoop underskirt. 1948 for Abraham & Strauss only. Also came in 14″ size.

12" "Pamela" shown in the window box she was sold in, in 1963. Two interchangeable wigs. Hard plastic doll. (Lissy). #1280 - Catalog reprint.

12" "Pamela" shown in carrying valise with 14-piece trousseau of 1963. Takes wigs (Lissy). #1285. Catalog reprint.

Pamela is a dainty, exquisite 12" doll, made of plastic and fully jointed with moving eyes. She comes packed in a roomy 20" carrying case with handle. Dressed in a lovely old-fashioned dress, Pamela has three additional party costumes in gay colors, including a ballerina outfit. Includes also a nightie, lingerie and accessories. In addition, Pamela keeps up with the latest in the fashion world by changing her wig. Included are blonde, platinum, and brunette wigs, with which her appearance is transformed for each party. Ship. wt. 6 lbs.

12" "Pamela Party Kit" in 20" carry case. Dressed in old-fashioned dress with three additional party costumes, ballerina outfit, nightie, lingerie and accessories. Sold for $25.00 in 1964 from the FAO Schwarz catalog.

PAMELA

CTORIA BABY DOLL 15
lressed in a delicate pink cotton dress with Irish l

1968 12" "Pamela" in an 18" case with peasant apron, nightie, lingerie. This FAO Schwarz item sold for $25.00 in their catalog.

9″ "Peasant". All composition with painted eyes to the side. Tagged. (Little Betty). All original. (Courtesy Jay Minter.)

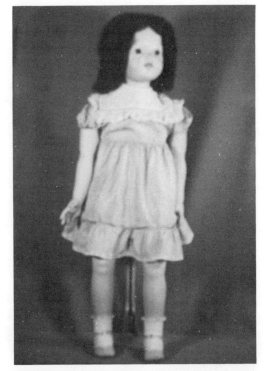

34″ "Penny". 1951. From comic strip about a teen-ager by Harry Haenigsen. Cloth body with stuffed vinyl, long "young girl-type" limbs. All fingers are long, separated and slender, with red polish. Glued on wig and painted brown eyes. Marks: Alexander on head. Not original.

PENNY

American cartoonist Harry Haenigsen was born in 1900 in New York City. He always had a flair for drawing and caricature, and in 1918 he joined the Bray animation studio as an assistant. In 1919 he enrolled at the Art Students League and at the same time was working as an art assistant on the *New York World*.

Harry Haenigsen's first comic strip was "Simeon Batts", which he created in 1922. This strip was about a radio buff and the havoc he created with his attempts at building crystal sets out of kitchen utensils and office furniture. By 1929 Haenigsen had developed a cartoon panel commenting on the daily news. This ran until 1931 when the *New York World* went out of business. Haenigsen then moved to the *New York Journal* and continued his "News and Views" panel. He was also an illustrator and worked for various magazines.

In 1937 Haenigsen went to work as story editor for Max Fleischer Studios, but returned to comic strips in 1938. He created "Our Bill" on March 6, 1939 for the *Herald-Tribune Syndicate*; this teen-age strip ran until 1966. His most memorable comic strip was "Penny", a replacement for Charles Voight's "Betty", which the *Tribune* had dropped. He originated "Penny" on June 20, 1943. "Penny" was one of the first "bobby-soxer" strips, and was about Penelope Mildred Pringle (Penny), her best friend Judy and members of the Pringle family. Well characterized, the plots were funny and the language up to date, but Haenigsen's graphic treatment was too elaborate, his close-ups, angle shots and scale distortions were too much of a distraction for what should have been a simple premise. In 1970 Haenigsen discontinued "Penny" and went into semi-retirement.

10½″ "Tiny Pinkie". Composition and cloth. Gauntlet hands, blue sleep eyes. Marks: Alexander, on head. Tag: Pinky Madame Alexander. 1937. (Courtesy Sharon Ivy)

11″ "Pinky Baby". All hard plastic with bent limb baby body and dimples in knees and hands. Cryer box in back. Painted lower lashes and sleep blue eyes. Original christening gown trimmed in blue ribbon, and blue crochet booties. The hair is molded. (Courtesy Dianne Hoffman)

CHART Page 151 for INDEX

17½″ "Polly On Tour" was a 1965 FAO Schwarz exclusive and cost $58.00 then. The metal trunk is 20″ with carry handle. White lace and tulle evening gown (wearing), blue taffeta cocktail dress, red velvet suit, pink tulle ballerina outfit, slippers, cotton slack set, figured cotton dress with petticoat, lace trimmed pink silk nightie, necklace, evening bag, straw hat, shoes, stockings and vanity set.

17″ "Polly" is shown in red velveteen suit, blouse, red shoes and bow. The clothes were for "Polly" and "Maria". (M) Tulle gown; (N) Blue Taffeta cocktail dress with evening jacket; (P) Red polka dot cotton dress with wide lace border at hem; (R) Lace trimmed crepe nightie; (S) Flowered nylon robe. This ad was in the 1965 FAO Schwarz catalog.

17″ "Polly" #1751-1965. Permanent pleated pink tulle skirt, with pink sequined bodice. (Courtesy Mary Williams)

25″ "Pitty Pat". Cloth clown with tag: Pitty Pat/Madame Alexander N.Y. U.S.A./All Rights Reserved. The owner, Judi Zemanek's mother, says an aunt in Philadelphia sent it to her sometime in the 1940's. To date, we have not been able to gather any information about this doll and outfit.

These two Madame Alexander poodles, "Za Za" and "Pierre", are 18″ tall and sold at Bullock's Wilshire. They were listed in an ad of November 1952 *House & Garden*. The dogs also came in a 14″ size.

1954 poodles made by Alexander Doll Co. They are 14″ tall, have plastic eyes and are tightly stuffed, with no moving parts. The Madame Alexander tag is glued on the bottom.

7″ "Polish" and so tagged. All composition with painted eyes to the side. Painted on shoes and socks. (Tiny Betty). (Courtesy Jay Minter)

16″, 22″ sizes of "Pollyanna" using the Marybel mold were made in 1960. Polished cotton dress with braid trimmed pinafore. Hair in pig-tails and high button shoes.

14″ "Polly Pigtails". 1949. (Maggie). All hard plastic. Dressed in yellow organdy dress with lace trim. Straw hat. Pigtails. Tag: Polly Pigtails/Madame Alexander, etc. (Courtesy Barbara Schilde)

20″ "Princess Alexandria". 1937. Cloth body with composition head and limbs. Sleep eyes and open mouth. Original. (Courtesy Barbara Schilde)

This 13″ Betty-faced "Princess Elizabeth" and trousseau sold for $10.75 in 1937 from a catalog of Emilie Pleydell of New York City called "The Shopper". The partitioned covered box measured 20″ x 24″. Besides the flower trimmed taffeta dress she is wearing, is a white dress, pink velvet coat and hat, red velvet evening wrap, cotton day dress, extra hat, shoes, pajamas, pearl necklace and jeweled head piece.

8″ "Princess Elizabeth". 1937. All composition and using the Dionne Quint head with painted blue eyes and mohair wig. The head is marked Dionne/Madame Alexander. The dress is tagged: Princess Elizabeth/Madame Alexander/All Rights Reserved. Replaced shoes. (Courtesy Nancy Roeder, photo by Susan Deats)

This outfit was offered in two sizes, 13″ and 18″ in the 1940 John Plain catalog. The blouse is white organdy and the skirt is pink organdy with shoulder straps embroidered with colorful petit point. White organdy lace trimmed slip and panties, white socks and black patent leather shoes.

LITTLE PRINCESS ELIZABETH
WITH A COMPLETE WARDROBE—AND TRUNK

Shown above, is the Royaldom of Dolldom, Princess Elizabeth and her complete wardrobe, carried in her own little trunk. The doll is 13½-in. size; the trunk is an airplane luggage type carrying case, complete even to travel labels. Just imagine how much fun you can have with the little Princess, dressing her in her morning play dress, her afternoon tea dress her party dress, and formal gown. She has a beautiful velvet cape, trimmed with real fur, the kind that all royalty wears; playsuit, housecoat, wide brimmed straw hat with flowers on it, extra pair of slippers, hose, handkerchiefs—everything exactly as pictured above, to make a most complete outfit. Princess Elizabeth has on a pearl necklace and golden tiara. She is really a darling, as sweet as can be—you can't resist her lovable face and sparkling eyes. This is the original and the only authentic Princess Elizabeth Doll.

N26452 Princess Elizabeth Outfit, Complete......................$14.50

13½" "Princess Elizabeth" in trunk that is an airplane luggage type, including travel labels. Her clothes include a morning play dress, afternoon tea dress, a party dress and formal gown. Has a velvet cape trimmed in real fur, playsuit, housecoat, straw hat with flowers, extra pair of slippers, hose, handkerchiefs. Doll wears a pearl necklace and golden tiara. This outfit sold for $14.95 in the 1940 John Plain Catalog.

16" "Princess Elizabeth" and 18" "Princess Margaret Rose". All composition and original. Princess Elizabeth is from 1937 and Princess Margaret Rose from 1947. (Courtesy Mary Williams)

19" "Princess Elizabeth". All composition with human hair wig, blue-green sleep eyes and open mouth. All original with original hair set. Marks: Princess Elizabeth Alexander Doll Co., on head. Tag: Princess Elizabeth/Madame Alexander NY/ All Rights Reserved. 1937. (Courtesy Glorya Woods)

13" Closed mouth "Princess Elizabeth". All composition (Betty). Blonde human hair wig, sleep eyes and slight dimple on left side of cheek. Marks: 13, on back. White taffeta gown, rose trim, red velvet cape with oval straw type hat. Red velvet trim and flowers at sides. Tag: Princess Elizabeth/Madame Alexander, etc. 1937. (Courtesy Sharon Ivy)

13″ "Princess Elizabeth". All composition, open mouth and sleep eyes. Original hair set and clothes. Both doll and clothes are marked and tagged. (Courtesy Marge Meisinger)

13″ "Princess Elizabeth". All composition with human hair wig, blue-green sleep eyes, closed mouth and dimples. All original pink gown with pink net trim on bodice and sleeves. Gold snap shoes. Tag: Princess Elizabeth/Madame Alexander NY/ All Rights Reserved. 1937. (Courtesy Glorya Woods)

15″ "Princess Elizabeth". All original with auburn mohair wig. Coat, hat and muff are blue faille fabric, dress is white organdy with blue dots. White fur trim. Marks: Princess Elizabeth /Mme. Alexander, on head. Tag: Madame/Alexander/New York USA. Doll is composition, open mouth and sleep eyes. 1937-1938. (Courtesy Glorya Woods)

14″ "Puddin'." Made one year in this size. #3730-1975. Vinyl with cloth body. Sleep eyes and rooted hair. Marks: Alexander/1975. (Courtesy Renie Culp)

24″ Wigged "Pumpkin". Cloth and vinyl with large painted eyes. Rooted hair over molded hair. Marks: Alexander/1967, on head. #9960-1976. (Courtesy Anita Pacey)

11″ "Toby". Hand puppet with composition head, fine cotton knit fabric body that is red, green scarf. Hands appear to be chamois. Tag, on back of neck, is printed in blue on white: Toby/Madame Alexander, N.Y. (Courtesy Gladys Brown)

FAO Schwarz, in 1966, carried this exclusive "Pussy Cat Doll Trousseau". 14″ doll in a wicker hamper that is 19″ x 11″ x 10″ with lift out tray. Doll wears a lace trimmed organdy dress and bonnet. Trousseau includes cotton play dress, Sunday smocked dress, checkered romper suit, flannel sleeper, diaper, corduroy coat/bonnet, knitted sacque and bonnet set. This outfit cost $55.00 in 1966.

This 1967 "Pussy Cat and Trousseau" is very much like the one made up in 1966 for FAO Schwarz and is in same size wicker case with lift out tray. The organdy dress the 14″ doll is wearing is different, as well as the pink dress with white bodice and sleeves that are checkered rather than plain.

14″ "Pussy Cat Trousseau" in FAO Schwarz catalog of 1968. Wicker hamper is 19″ x 11″ x 10″ with lift out tray. Dressed in a lace trimmed organdy dress under pink pleated coat and hat. Clothes include a cotton play dress, a Sunday polka-dot dress, sunsuit, two-piece creeper set, flannel sleeper and extra diaper, a bunting with bonnet, rattle, brush, comb and towel set. This item cost $63.00 in 1967.

The 1969 FAO Schwarz "Pussy Cat" was still 14″ tall and came in the same wicker hamper case with lift out tray. This year wardrobe included candy striped party dress with matching bonnet, two-piece sleeper set, white and yellow checkered play dress with matching bloomers, pink flannel bunting and bonnet.

The "Pussy Cat Trousseau" of 1970 for Schwarz is still in the wicker hamper case with lift out tray and the clothes include a lace trimmed cotton Sunday dress with matching bonnet, a play dress with matching bloomers, flowered flannel nightie and satin trimmed flannel bunting with matching hood, a terry cloth robe, towel and washcloth. The cost of this outfit in 1970 was $65.00.

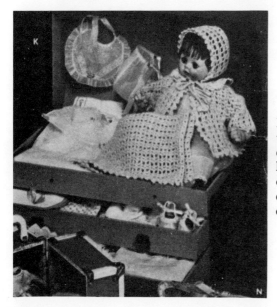

Marshall Field sold the Alexander doll as "Cynthia" for an unbelievable price of $395.00! The doll is 20″ and had ten outfits besides the dress, hand crocheted sweater, bonnet and matching coverlet. All fit into the two drawer, Napoleonic dome top trunk by Louis Vuitton. This was an exclusive with Marshall Field. 1970.

P
Q

$68.50 in 1971, this "Pussy Cat Trousseau" included the wicker hamper case with lift out tray, nylon party dress, lace trimmed cotton Sunday dress with matching bonnet, play dress with matching bloomers, flowered flannel nightie and satin trimmed flannel bunting with hood.

24″ "Pussy Cat". #6560-1971. Cloth body with vinyl head and limbs. Sleep eyes and rooted hair. Marks: Alexander/1965, on head. (Courtesy Renie Culp)

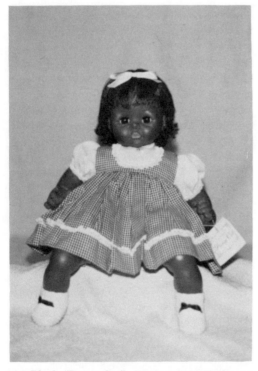

20″ Black "Pussy Cat". #5140-1976. Cloth and vinyl. Sleep eyes and rooted hair. Marks: Alexander/1965, on head. 20″ still being made, 1976 was last year for the 14″ size. (Courtesy Renie Culp)

21″ "Queen Elizabeth". #2170-1961. All hard plastic with one-piece vinyl arms. Uses same doll as the 1961 Sleeping Beauty. The Cissy doll used for the "Queen" (#2180-1962) has a gold brocade gown with very small flowers. (Courtesy Mary Williams)

14" older "Rebbeca". #1485-1968 and 1969. The change took place in 1970 with the doll having a one-piece skirt with lace hem trim, lace yoke (no buttons) and tulle trimmed poke bonnet. All in pink.

12" "Romeo and Juliet". Plastic and vinyl, blue sleep eyes and brunette hair. He: red stretch tights, purple velvet jacket, powder blue hat with red feather and brown felt slippers. She: ivory color chiffon gown, cap of gold mesh with seed pearls, iridescent vest with gold trim, gold slippers. (Courtesy Susan Rogers)

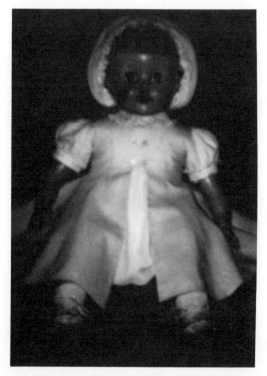

25" "Rosebud" shown in #7561-1952. Cloth and early vinyl with sleep eyes and molded hair. (Courtesy Doris Richardson)

16" "Rosebud" #3561-1952. Fashion Academy Award medal came with doll. This dress also came in red. There were also sizes 19" and 23". Cloth with vinyl head and limbs. Molded hair. (Courtesy Doris Richardson)

15″ "Rosamund Bridesmaid". #1551-1953. Also came in 18″ size (#1851). Hard plastic walker (Maggie). All original with light tan gown and olive green band hat with pink flowers. Also came in pink and yellow. (Courtesy Beth Donar)

21″ "Rosey-Posey". #6790-1976. Cloth with vinyl head and limbs. Sleep eyes and rooted hair. Marks: Alexander/1965, on head. Made one year only. (Courtesy Renie Culp)

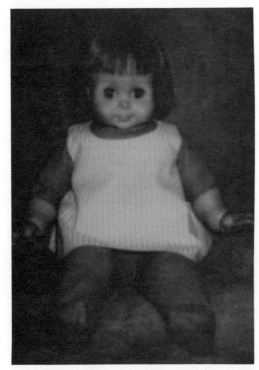

11″ "Scarlett O'Hara". All composition with green sleep eyes and black wig. All original in taffeta dress. Is in original box. 1939. (Courtesy Marge Meisinger)

20″ "Rusty" #5260-1967. Cloth and vinyl. Red rooted hair and sleep eyes. Freckles. Had ribbon bows on each side of head and black patent pumps. (Courtesy Doris Richardson)

21″ "Scarlett O'Hara". 1940. All composition with black wig and green sleep eyes. Gown is brown taffeta with green ribbon tie, hat and trim. White pleated organdy collar. (Courtesy Mary Williams)

18″ Elise as "Scarlett O'Hara". Black hair. Organdy gown trimmed in lace with rosebuds. Very large picture hat. Jointed ankles and knees. 1963. #1760. Catalog reprint.

21″ "Scarlett" of 1978. Plastic and vinyl with green sleep eyes, brunette hair. Rose printed satin gown with green parasol. Natural straw picture hat trimmed with roses. Green high heeled shoes. (Courtesy Rita DiMare)

Marshall Field had this 14″ Alexander baby exclusive during 1971 and the doll was called "Serena". Doll came with a fourteen outfit layette and accessories. The trunk is described as "velvety". This item sold for $150.00 in 1971.

S

Shari Lewis was an extremely popular ventriloquist and puppeteer on T.V. This photo is of the back cover of "The Shari Lewis Puppet Book", published in 1958.

14" "Shari Lewis" #1430-1959 in original skirt and blouse. This doll is rather unique, and in the owner's own words (Bessie Carson) is as follows: "The owner of the store where I often bought dolls, told me I should buy this one as it was a novelty doll and wouldn't be on the market long. Then she said the Alexander salesman had just come in for her order, and as she was low on dolls, she asked to buy some of his samples. Her store was the last stop on his route, so he granted her request. This Shari Lewis was one of those dolls, and head is "clear" hard plastic and not painted over, the eyes are hazel, not bright green, her shoes are light blue, not gold as were the later ones. She does not have jewelry, nor did she have a box." (Courtesy Bessie Carson)

21" "Shari Lewis" of 1959 is modeling a pink penoir and gown for Cissy also boxed extra. (Courtesy Charmaine Shields)

This photo shows the body of "Sitting Pretty" #5620-1965. Foam body and limbs with gauntlet vinyl hands. Blue sleep eyes. Marks: Alexander 1965, on head. (Courtesy Jaime Pendlebury)

18″ "Sitting Pretty" #5620-1965. Foam body and limbs, wired so she can be posed. Vinyl head and gauntlet hands. Sleep blue eyes and rooted hair. One of the rarest Alexander baby dolls. (Courtesy Doris Richardson)

16½″ "Sleeping Beauty" doll undressed, so the body and extra joints can be seen. (Courtesy Lilah M. Beck)

17″ Walt Disney "Sleeping Beauty" using the Elise doll. #1895-1959. Hard plastic and fully jointed. (Courtesy Mary Williams)

16″ "Snow White". All composition with black mohair wig, sleep eyes and open mouth. (Princess Elizabeth). Clothes are pale yellow. Tag: Snow White/Madame Alexander NY/USA/All Rights Reserved. (Courtesy Marge Meisinger)

12″ "Snow White". All composition and original. Was Christmas doll of 1939 for owner, Margaret Mandel. All composition with bent right arm, glued on black mohair wig, sleep brown eyes/lashes and bright red nail polish. She wears white pantalettes (just to mid-calf), white socks and leatherette shoes with round heels and rose bow. Marks: Pr. Elizabeth/Alexander, on head. Tag: Snow White/Madame Alexander NY/All Rights Reserved (Blue print on white tag) (Courtesy Margaret Mandel)

21″ "Snow White" in satin and velvet. (Margaret). All hard plastic. The 21″ size was made in 1949 and 1950. 15″ and 23″ in 1951 and 15″, 18″ and 23″ in 1952. (Courtesy Sandra Crane)

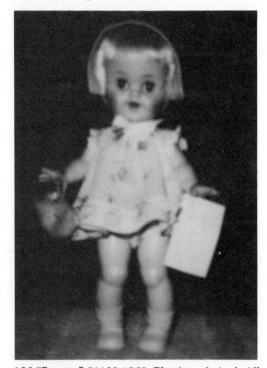

12″ "Smarty" #1132-1962. Plastic and vinyl. All original. (Courtesy Doris Richardson)

This "Artie and Smartie Trousseau" was listed in the FAO Schwarz catalog in 1962, along with "Katie and Tommie", the anniversary dolls, but this set is not listed as being exclusive. The dolls are 12″, and the "model" case of blue leatherette is 14″. "Artie" is in blue serge pants, white shirt and red jacket and has a play suit in cotton with blue checkered shirt, blue shorts and blue pajamas. "Smartie" is dressed in lace trimmed nylon dress, matching panties, poke hat and flower basket. She also has blue cotton play dress with striped panties and pink nightie. Included were brush and comb sets, sunglasses, mirror, badminton set.

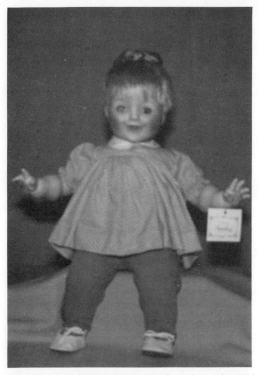

20″ "Smiley" #5585-1971. Cloth body with vinyl head and limbs. Rooted hair and sleep eyes. Wide open/closed mouth. Marks: Alexander/1970, on head. (Courtesy Renie Culp)

13″ "Sonja Henie" in original red velvet skating outfit. Tag: Genuine Sonja Henie. All composition. 1939. (Courtesy Linda Crowsey)

14″ "Sonja Henie". All composition. 1940. Shown in original case with wardrobe. The white dress with rosebuds on it has a gold paper tag at the hem that says: Sonja Henie. (Courtesy Mimi Hiscox)

14″ "Sonja Henie". All composition with open mouth and four teeth. Blonde mohair wig in original set with cluster of flowers, dimples and brown eyes. All original dress of orange silk and organdy with rows of tiny raised stars. 1940. Tag: Sonja Henie Mme. Alexander/All Rights Reserved, etc. Mme Alexander/Sonja Henie, on head. (Courtesy Rita DiMare)

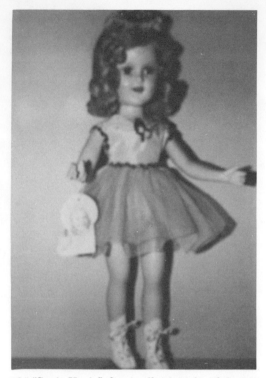

18″ "Sonja Henie". All composition. Doll is un-marked. Dress tag: A Genuine Sonja Henie Doll/Madame Alexander, etc. Arm tag bears likeness of Sonja and her signature. (Courtesy Barbra Jean Male, photo by Michael Male)

18″ "Sonja Henie" that is all original with brown sleep eyes and open mouth. All composition with cheek dimples. Hair is in original set. Marks: Madame Alexander/Sonja Henie, on head. Ge-nuine/Sonja Henie Doll/ Madame Alexander/All Rights Reserved. 1939. (Courtesy Glorya Woods)

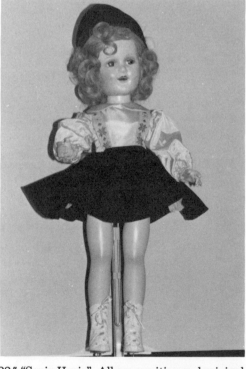

21″ "Sonja Henie". All composition and original. Dressed in black velvet with gold trim. 1939. (Courtesy Mary Williams)

22″ "Sonja Henie". All composition and original. Open mouth/six teeth. Velvet skirt and satin blouse. Velvet hat. Tag: Genuine Sonja Henie Doll/All Rights Reserved. Marks: Madame Alex-ander Sonja Henie, on head. (Courtesy Rosemary Meyecic)

This Lissy is dressed in the "Sound Of Music" sailor suit that is shown in the wrist booklet, although this doll does not have the FIRST booklet. (Courtesy Glorya Woods)

17" "Maria". (Polly). Original except apron and hat are missing. Alexander ad of 1965 reads, "To personify governess Maria, (Julie Andrews) Madame Alexander has created a new beautiful 17" doll". The doll Polly using the Maria mold was introduced in 1965 also. Tag: Maria from "The Sound Of Music"/Madame Alexander. Head is marked: Alexander Doll Co./1965. (Courtesy Margaret Mandel)

There are two originally dressed dolls, and both are "Brigitta" from the large "Sound of Music" set. The smaller one is a Lissy and the larger one is a Mary Ann-faced doll. Just as sometimes the Elise, or the Polly were used for the Marias, Lissy was also used for "Brigitta". (Courtesy Sandra Crane)

12" Friedrich of "Sound of Music" using the Smarty mold instead of the more common Janie mold. (Courtesy Sherry Kraft)

15″ "Southern Girl". 1940. All composition. (Wendy Ann). Gown is cream colored taffeta with floral design and has green velvet bows and trim. Pantaloons and wire hooped slip. Green shoes. (Courtesy Mildred Hightower)

"Southern Girl" of 1942-43 (after "Gone With The Wind" movie had "died down"). Composition, black wig and either blue or green eyes. Came in sizes: 11″-15″-18″ and 22″. The 15″ also came with a taffeta coat (full length) and bonnet to match. Catalog reprint.

10″ "Southern Belle" with yellow ribbon trim. Hard plastic with bend-knees. (Cissette) #1170-1968. Green sleep eyes and brown hair. Tag: Southern Belle by Madame Alexander. (Courtesy Sharon Ivy)

7″ "Spanish". All composition with side painted eyes and black mohair wig. Painted on black shoes. Tag: Spanish/Madame Alexander, etc. (Courtesy Jay Minter)

9″ "Spanish" boy and girl. (Little Betty). All composition with painted eyes to the side. 1937-1938. (Courtesy LaDonna Dolan)

15″ "Story Princess" #1549-1955 only with variation of tiara and bodice trim. Pink taffeta. One shown in catalog has sequined tiara and trim. In 1954 the "Story Princess" also had the Margaret face, but had a self-material stole collar and a top skirt that came half way down over floor length gown, with edges caught up with roses. Came in 15″ and 18″ sizes. In 1956 there was an 8″ size, as well as 15″ and 18″ using the Cissy face. (Courtesy Barbara Schilde)

25″ "Story Princess" walker. All hard plastic. Shown in the 1955 Montgomery Ward catalog. The Cissy face was used also for "Binnie" and "Winnie Walker".

14″ "Lively Sugar Darlin'." All original. Came in pink box. #3525-1964. Cloth and vinyl. (Courtesy Doris Richardson)

In the FAO Schwarz catalog of 1964 "Sugar Tears" in this wicker basket sold for $50.00. The hamper is 19″ x 11″ x 10″ and has lift out tray. Came with toddler dress with matching panties. Included lace trimmed organdy dress with petticoat, pink Sunday dress, heart decorated play dress, flannel sleeper, extra diapers, hooded bunting and sacque, bonnet and bootie set, bib, brush and comb, rattle and bottle.

16″ "Susie Q" as shown in the 1940 John Plain catalog. Her dress is cloth and the jacket is felt. All cloth body and yellow yarn hair. Painted features. 1940.

13″ "Susie Q" and "Bobby Q". All original with Bobby carrying a book and Susie a small black umbrella. All cloth bodies with cotton and felt clothes, painted faces and yarn hair. Note that the eyes are painted to the sides and Susie's are to the left and Bobby's are to the right. 1940. Tag: Susie Q by Madame Alexander NY All Rights Reserved. Bobby Q reads the same. Original box. (Courtesy Rosemary Meyecic)

9″ "Sweden" of 1935-1938. All composition with painted eyes to the side. (Little Betty). Variation of suspenders attached to one-piece suit. (Courtesy LaDonna Dolan)

9″ "Swedish". 1935-1938. All composition. (Little Betty). Short blonde mohair wig. One-piece suit with red fake garters at knees. Green trimmed ruffles down front and green satin bow at neck. White eyelet cuff and collar with black sleeves to simulate blouse. Long white stockings. Green straw hat with small white and red poms. Tag: Swedish. Marks: Mme Alexander New York, on back. (Courtesy Kathleen Rudisill)

9″ "Sweet Tears". 1965 to 1974. All vinyl. Was discontinued, in this size, in 1974. (Courtesy Renie Culp)

14″ All vinyl "Sweet Tears". Tagged pink organdy dress trimmed with white lace. High cheek coloring. Doll marked: Alexander 1965. 12″ All vinyl "Sweet Tears" with pupiless black eyes. Pink and white polka dot dress. Marked: Alexander 65. (Courtesy Margaret Mandel)

D 811-10 (
(1
Cute as can
three in sof
white check
wicker bask
Mother with
while puppie
bows have l

Ⓔ E 8
Appe
ham
white
organ
sleep

G 803-111 SEWING BASKET ....
(7 yrs. up)—Young dressmakers have the fun and satisfaction of

This "Sweet Tears Trousseau" cost $50.00 in 1965 at the FAO Schwarz store and is listed as an exclusive. The doll is 16″. The wicker case with lift out tray is 19″ x 11″ x 10″. She wears a pink and white dotted dress with lace trimmed petticoat. Clothes include a lace trimmed organdy dress with slip, a pink "Sunday best" dress, pink checkered cotton romper, flannel sleeper and extra diaper. Also she has hooded bunting and knit sacque and bonnet set, brush, comb, rattle, bottle and pacifier.

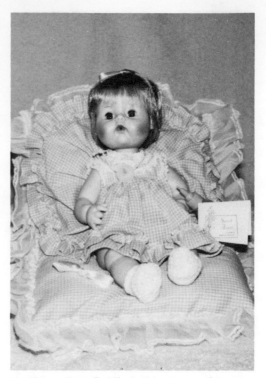

14″ "Sweet Tears" as shown in the 1967 FAO Schwarz catalog. Wears sheer cotton dress with lace trim, has party dress, coat with matching bonnet and toys to "keep her busy". Sold for $16.95.

14″ "Sweet Tears". All vinyl, open mouth/nurser. All original. #3730-1967. Came with pink/white check pillow. 14″ still available. Discontinued in 9″ size. Marks: Alexander/1965, on head. (Courtesy Renie Culp)

Marshall Field exclusive in 1970 was the "Sweet Tears" in wicker basket with nine outfits and selling for $44.95.

During 1971 the Marshall Field Company offered this exclusive "Sweet Tears" (13″) in a wicker hamper. There were eight outfits. The cost in 1970 was $44.95.

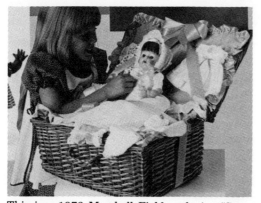

This is a 1973 Marshall Field exclusive "Sweet Tears" in wicker basket. This 14″ doll and outfit cost $44.95 in 1973.

9″ "Sweet Tears". Open mouth/nurser, sleep eyes, all vinyl with painted hair. Discontinued in 1975. (Courtesy Barbara Schilde)

13″ "Sweet Tears" #3632-1976-77. All vinyl in white organdy christening gown. Three rows of lace down skirt, lace on hem and large lace trimmed collar. White satin bow with long streamers at bodice line. White organdy bonnet trimmed with ruffle lace. Pacifier around neck and plastic baby bottle tied to wrist. Marks: Alexander 1965, on head. Tag: Sweet Tears. (Courtesy Kathleen Rudisill)

22″ "Sweetie Baby" wearing an organdy dress and matching, bonnet lace trimmed. 1962. #6940. (Courtesy Doris Richardson)

"Sweet Violet" came in 18″ size only (1954). Jointed at elbows and knees. This dress is polished cotton with contrasting yoke. Came in various colors. Catalog reprint.

18″ "Sweet Violet" of 1954 shown in pink fille coat over a pink taffeta dress with ruffle at hem line. The hat and bag are moss green velvet and shoes are pink suede. Catalog reprint. Jointed wrist.

Left: The current Thailand "face", introduced during 1977 shown along with the 1973 to 1977 "face". (Courtesy Anita Pacey)

8″ "Swiss Girl" of 1962 with the Maggie Mix-up face. Bend knees. All original. (Courtesy Pat Spirek)

TONY SARG

Tony Sarg was born in Guatemala in 1880 (died 1940). The son of a German consul, he grew up to become a highly successful illustrator in London. Tony Sarg built up a collection of old toys and acquired an interest in marionettes. He studied with the famous Holden troupe, then moved on to produce his own studio shows, one of which was seen by George Bernard Shaw. In 1915, he moved to New York and teamed up with two other illustrators Frank Godwin and Mat Searle. Their first big touring show was an adaptation of Washington Irving's "Rip Van Winkle". Among other outstanding activities, Tony Sarg invented the animated gas-filled creatures for the Macy Parade. He authored a book with Anne Stoddard called "Book of Marionette Plays".

Tony Sarg was the leading man in puppetry by the 1930's. His largest show was at the Chicago Fair in 1933. It was seen by more than three million people and it was then that industry was beginning to use puppetry for advertising and public relations.

In March of 1934 it was reported in Playthings Magazine that a line of Tony Sarg Marionettes were available along with a theatre. The SPONSOR (not the manufacturer or maker, but distributor) of the Marionettes and theatre was the Alexander Doll Co. By June 1937 the Playthings ads were reading, "How natural for Madame Alexander to collaborate with this famed artist in the design and construction of this beautiful line" (marionettes). The ads show the 11 plays that were available with 33 characters: "Hansel and Gretel" (Hansel, Gretel and witch), "Rip Van Winkle" (Rip, Dame, Judith), "Alice in Wonderland" (Alice, Humpty, T. Dee & T. Dum), "Tingling Circus #1" (Clown Zaza, Dog Fido), "Tingling Circus #2" (Riding Master-Percival, Ballet Dancer, Horse). It is interesting to note the Twinkling Circus by September ads. "Dixie Land Minstrels" (Sambo, Bones & Interlocutor), "The Enchanted Prince" (Prince, Princess, Gnome pumpet), "The Three Wishes" (Martin, Margaret, Fairy Titania), "Lucy Lavender's Hero" (Lucy Lawrence, Butler Tippytoes), "Clever Gretchen" (Gretchen & Mr. Archibald), "Red Riding Hood" (Red, Grandmother & Wolf).

The Playthings Magazine carried ads during 1938 for EXCLUSIVE with Madame Alexander, the Walt Disney marionette. The first of these was Snow White and the Seven Dwarfs. The "Silly Symphony" Theatre (Disney) could be purchased with Minnie and Mickey Mouse and the complete cast of Show White. Donald Duck and Pluto were also available.

7½" "Tiny Betty". 1935. All composition with painted eyes to side and painted on shoes and socks. Original. Tag: Madame Alexander New York. Pink dotted swiss dress. (Courtesy Barbara Schilde)

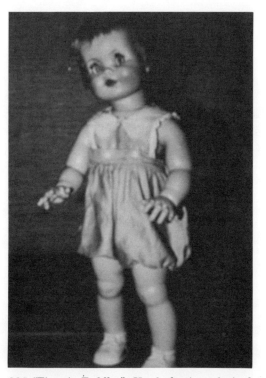

23" "Timmie Toddler". Hard plastic and vinyl. Flirty eyes. #7732-1960. Shown in original romper. Marks: Alexander Doll/1960, on head. "Mama" voice box in back. (Courtesy Janine Chalstrom)

and
TONY SARG

Youngsters and a d u l t s— erybody enjoys these mari- ettes! These are authentic pies of Tony Sarg and Walt sney characters, beloved by ung and old alike through- t the world. All are beau- ully finished in bright, dur- le colors, lifelike to the allest detail. Each marion- te averages a foot in height d is easy to manipulate. ey have patented stringing d mounting and are all set , ready to operate. Walt sney characters i n c l u d e ickey and Minnie Mouse, onald Duck and Pluto, Snow hite and the Seven Dwarfs. ony Sarg characters include ttle Red Riding Hood, The g Bad Wolf, Hansel and retel, Tweedledee and Twee- edum, Alice in Wonderland d The Clown. For complete ts, see choice of theatres at ft.

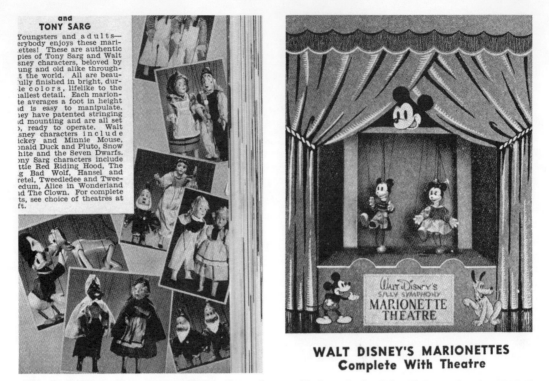

WALT DISNEY'S MARIONETTES
Complete With Theatre

This Disney theatre was 38" x 47½" in size and was sold through the John Plain catalog for 1940. It and two marionettes listed for $14.20, four marionettes $19.50 and eight marionettes for 23.50. See

This theatre measures 32" x 51" set up. It was sold with two marionettes for $14.20, four marionettes for $19.50 or eight marionettes for $29.50 in the 1940 John Plain Catalog.

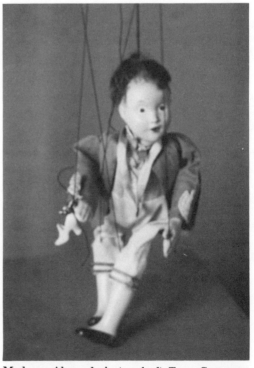

Madame Alexander's (marked) Tony Sarg pup- pet, "Prince Charming". He carries a slipper in one hand. Courtesy Mariann's Doll House (Billie McCabe).

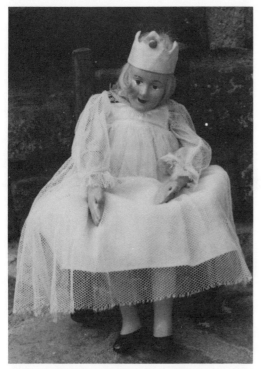

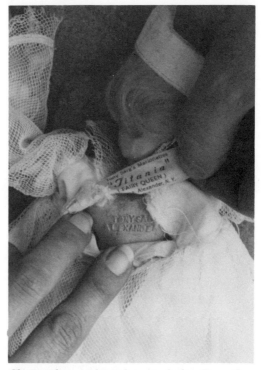

12″ Tony Sarg marionette with composition head, hands and legs with painted on shoes. Original. Marks: Tony Sarg/Alexander, on shoulder. From the play "The Three Wishes". Tag: Tony Sarg's Marionettes/Titania/(Fairy Queen)/Madame Alexander, N.Y. (Courtesy Mimi Hiscox)

Shows the mark and tag of the Tony Sarg marionette Titania the Fairy Queen. From the play "The Three Wishes". Two other marionettes, "Martin" and "Margaret", make up the play. (Courtesy Mimi Hiscox)

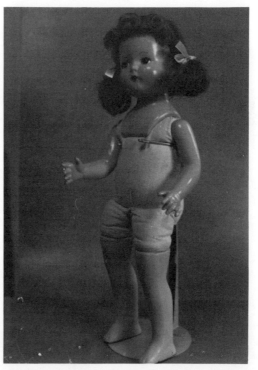

This Tony Sarg, (marked Alexander) puppet is dressed as a girl scout. (Courtesy Mariann's Doll House, Billie McCabe)

17″ Composition head on shoulder plate, bent composition arms and straight legs. Cloth body. Brown sleep eyes/lashes. Cryer in body. Marked: Alexander, on head. There is no way to tell who this doll is because there are no original clothes. (Courtesy Janine Chalstrom)

12″ Painted-eye baby of 1943 and 1944. (Due to WWII, the supply of eyes ran out). This baby could be "Butch", "Baby Genius" or "Precious", but because it has no original clothes, it is impossible to tell. Composition head and limbs. Cloth body, mohair wig over molded hair. (Courtesy Mimi Hiscox)

18″ Unknown. We do not know if she was meant to be a bride, or what. (Sleeping Beauty). Gown is in two pieces. Bottom wraps around, top and slip attached. Two rows of nylon tulle ruffles at hem. Marks: Alexander, on head. Tag: Madame Alexander/New York U.S.A. 1959. (Courtesy Sharon Ivy)

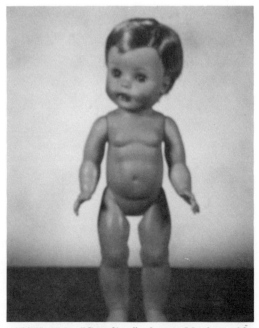

It is not known if the Madame Alexander Doll Co. had purposed this doll to go with the large "Sound of Music" set or not. It is a Caroline doll with a boy's haircut. A number of the dolls (nude) were sold to a New York firm (Doll Craft & World) in 1978. These "sample" outfits were sold to a mid-west store. They fit, but appeared to be slightly altered in a rear seam. Pants are navy, with Tyrolean-style suspenders. Jacket is red. They are "Alexander quality".

13½″-14″ "Caroline" boy. Marks: Alexander/1961, on head and Alexander/13 on back. All vinyl with sleep eyes and rooted hair. Has same basic hairdo as the Caroline, but in boy cut. These dolls were sample stock and never actually put on the market. There is no basis for the rumor that was supposed to be "John-John" (Kennedy), but there may be a basis to the idea that he was meant to be part of the large "Sound of Music" set "Kurt". (Courtesy Pat Gardner)

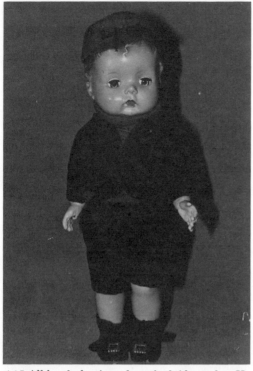

14″ All hard plastic and marked Alexander. Has the Lovey Dovey head. Part of clothes may be original. Ca. 1949-1952. (Courtesy Marjorie Uhl)

18″ Walker. (Margaret) The gown #210-1952 was sold extra. Tag: 18″ tall Madame Alexander Fashions. The tag is located sewn in the dress at the waist in the back. Pink gown with black trim. This same dress was also sold in a 15″ size and tagged: 15″ tall. (Courtesy Paula Ryscik)

18″ Unknown all hard plastic with the Maggie face. Dress is unmarked, but looks factory made. Hair is most unusual as it is in tiny braids. Ca. 1950-1952. (Courtesy Susan Goetz)

18″ Maggie-faced unknown doll. Shows the tiny braids around back of head. It may be suggested that this doll is one of the Little Women with loop curls, but the curls are actually "looped" and not braided on the "Amy" of the Little Women group, plus "Amy" was always a blonde. (Courtesy Susan Goetz)

14″ Maggie face. Unknown. All hard plastic with brown sleep eyes. Has loose curl, very black caracul wig. Clothes may not be original. (Courtesy Mary Partridge)

21″ Unknown Portrait. Production sample that was purchased by a buyer at the Toy Fair in New York City in 1974. Came in the regular portrait box with the Alexander label but there is no name, nor number. (Courtesy Betty Snider)

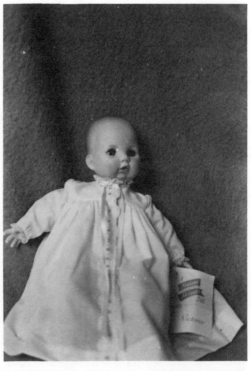

19″ "Victoria" with rooted hair. Ca. 1972. Cloth body with vinyl head and limbs. Nothing is known about this doll, and she does not appear in the Alexander catalogs. (Courtesy Betty Motsinger)

14″ "Victoria". Cloth and vinyl head and limbs. Spray painted hair, sleep eyes. #3746-1975 and made to date. The very first doll was 18″ tall (1966), and a 20″ size was made from 1967 to date. The 18″ size was re-introduced again in 1978. (Courtesy Barbara Schilde)

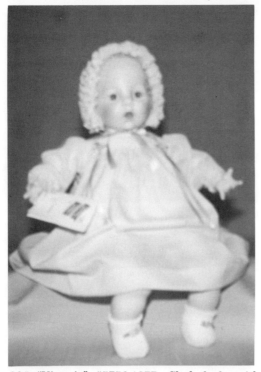

20″ "Victoria" #5756-1977. Cloth body with vinyl head and limbs. Spray painted hair and sleep eyes. Marks: Alexander/1973, on head. (Courtesy Renie Culp)

11″ "Wendy Ann". All composition. All original except shoes. Has a most unusual hairdo in that the curls are so large and tied at the ends. Tag: Wendy Ann Madame Alexander N.Y. Doll is unmarked. 1936. (Courtesy Lilah Beck)

14″ "Wendy Ann". 1940. All composition with blonde wig and brown sleep eyes. Original cotton dress. Swivel waist. Bent elbow on right arm. Marks: Wendy Ann/Mme. Alexander/New York, on back. Dress tagged: Wendy Ann/Madame Alexander. (Courtesy Mary Sweeney)

13½″ "Wendy Ann". All composition and original. Shown with original box that has a different end paper with different views of Wendy Anns. Came with a mink coat and muff tagged: Bartelsbeck Fur Co. Mfg. Furriers-Cleveland, O. 1936. (Courtesy Marge Meisinger)

14″ "Wendy Ann". All composition and all original. Dress is pink organdy and note lace "half" gloves. Blonde human hair wig, swivel waist, closed mouth and sleep eyes. Marks: Wendy-Ann/Mme. Alexander/New York, on back. Tag: Wendy Ann/by Madame Alexander N.Y./All Rights Reserved. Gold colored wrist tag: Created/by/Madame Alexander/New York. Reverse side: An/Alexander/Product/Supreme/ Quality and/Design. 1945. (Courtesy Glorya Woods)

14″ "Wendy Ann" of 1950. All hard plastic. (Margaret). Auburn mohair wig, white organdy dress with yellow rick-rack trim. (Courtesy Sharon Ivy)

"Wendy Ann" of 1952, 1953 and 1954 came in this dress. #412 School Dress. Came in 15″, 18″ and 25″ sizes. Red/navy blue plaid, or red/green plaid. (Margaret). All hard plastic. (Courtesy Paula Ryscik)

15″ "Winnie Walker". (Cissy). All hard plastic, walker and head turns. Flat feet. #1534-1953. (Courtesy Barbara Schilde)

This "Winnie Walker Trousseau" was listed as an exclusive at FAO Schwarz in 1953 and cost $22.50. 15″ doll of hard plastic and is a walker. Wears an organdy dress and case contains a nightie, flannel coat and beret, taffeta dress, panties, straw hat, jewel case, gloves, bath slippers, bathing suit, socks, curlers, combs and a basket of flowers.

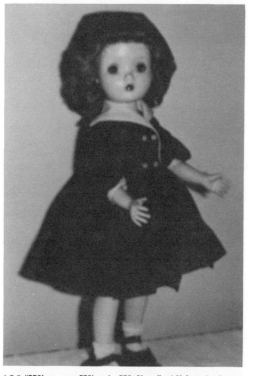

18″ "Winsome Winnie Walker". All hard plastic. 1953. Brown wig, bluish green sleep eyes. #1836. Red sleeveless taffeta dress, navy cloth coat with matching hat. Tag: Winnie Walker/Mme. Alexander, etc. Alexander, on head. (Courtesy Rita DiMare)

"Winsome Winnie Walker" came in sizes 15″, 18″ and 24″. 1953. Flat footed, uses Cissy face and is a walker. This dress is organdy with lace and pearl buttons. Catalog reprint.

This doll was an exclusive with the FAO Schwarz stores during 1953. She came in 25″ size only and is a hard plastic walker (Winnie-Binnie). Dressed in blue taffeta coat and bonnet, over a party dress of shell pink taffeta. The bonnet is trimmed with ostrich plume and pink rosebuds. Her shoes are blue. Also has hat box and white gloves. Her cost in 1953 was $22.00.

15″ "Winsome Winnie Walker" of 1953. The white dress and hat are pique cotton and the coat is red taffeta. (The opposite combination of materials are in the 1953 catalog discription). (Courtesy Pam Ortman)

18″ "Winsome Winnie Walker" #1822-1954. All hard plastic. (Cissy face). (Courtesy Sharon Ivy)

18″ "Wendy Bride" #1851-1955. Hard plastic with vinyl oversleeved arms. (Margaret). (Courtesy Mary Williams)

8″ Bend knee "Yugoslavia" with polka dot stockings. Again it must be pointed out that variations did, and do occur. (Courtesy Renie Culp)

COMPARISON STUDY

If you are a major Madame Alexander doll collector, then you must teach yourself all the telltale signs of a true Alexander doll. You must become aware of the little things that yell "Alexander" to you. You must become so familiar with your subject that you can pick up a doll and immediately accept or reject it. This takes time, study and patience, and particularly a sense of dedication, a second nature of a detective, and the ability to "grin and bear" it if you should make a mistake. To be able to accept YOURSELF when you accidently buy a wrong doll is so important. You see, your anger is really directed at yourself, although verbally you may be whopping mad at the person that sold you the doll . . . the mainstream theme of your anger is that YOU were so dumb to allow it to happen to you, therefore you vent your emotions on others. (Here I am talking about buying a doll AFTER you have seen it, not by mail-order and un-seen).

I used to stop at show tables and tell them they were selling as an Alexander something entirely different. It did not take me long to realize I only caused people to get mad and I stopped doing that. I now just keep my fingers crossed that the dolls remain unsold! Dealers, full or part time ones, should not sell a doll as an Alexander without studying the Alexanders well enough to know what they are doing. It is not so important in other areas of modern doll collecting, because the prices are not so high, and it doesn't hurt as much to make a mistake.

The prices of the Madame Alexander dolls are based ONLY on the demand for the dolls. Supply versus demand has always been with us, and there are far more collectors of these fine dolls, than there are dolls . . . so each step of the way, the prices increase and increase and increase. I often think about the young collector, the house-wife on limited budget, the retired person who can ill afford to over-spend, and it really disturbs me when any one of them get stuck with non-Alexander, at an Alexander price. That is the reason for the following comparison study. If it helps one person, then the time and work getting it together was well worth the trouble.

Madame Alexander has always been a business woman, but she has also always been a humanitarian. This part of her made the decision during 1949 to allow American Character, Arranbee and Madame Alexander Doll Company to all work from the White Plains, N.Y. factory with the introduction and acceptance of hard plastics. All three companies shared the same body and limb molds. American Character's Sweet Sues and the Arranbee's Nanettes were very, very similar. It is important, you the collector, can tell the difference. Don't feel bad if you have purchased one of these dolls as an Alexander, as their quality is high and ALL hard plastics are very collectable . . . after all, all of them are nearly 25 years old already.

Success is always copied, and to some this is a compliment. In the toy and doll area, it is business. There must have been at least thirty copies of the Shirley Temple doll, at least 10 copies of the Dionne Quints, so it should not surprise us that there were "copies", "Look a likes", or whatever of the highly accepted and desirable Madame Alexander dolls of the 1950's. Also we must take into account this fact . . . the 1950's was an era of the "BEAUTIFUL" doll. No other ten year span can touch the beauty of the dolls, themselves, quality wise, nor the costuming that went on during this period. Each company seemed to try and outdo the other, with Madame in the lead.

Close-up of the face of the Nanette by Arranbee and the Alexander-Margaret-face doll. This comparison should help in identity, as the Nanette has a more pointed chin and the eyes are cut out larger.

All hard plastic dolls. The two dark-headed ones are marked 14, on the heads and Made in U.S.A., on the backs. The blonde is marked Madame Alexander Margaret doll and is used to show that they all appear to be identical. There is no information about these 14″ dolls as yet. (Courtesy Mickey Canan and Mary Partridge)

14″ Margaret-face Alexander doll shown with an Arranbee Nanette. The bodies and limbs are identical. Both dolls are non-walkers.

This close-up between the blonde Margaret doll by Madame Alexander, and the doll like her that is marked 14, on head and Made in U.S.A. on the back, look very much alike, with this exception . . . the lashes are painted much longer and heavier on the dolls marked "14". When the Margaret molds were sold by Alexander Doll Co., it is not known who bought them.

This is a comparision study of the hands of an Alexander Cissy (Binnie or Winnie Walker) and a Sweet Sue all hard plastic walker by American Character. The bodies and limbs are identical.

Shows the identical bodies and limbs of an Alexander walker and a Sweet Sue walker.

14″ Marked 14, on the head and Made in USA, on the back. All hard plastic with rosy cheeks and extra long painted lashes. All original gown, hat and parasol that is not of Alexander quality. Maker of the doll is unknown. (Courtesy Mary Partridge)

The following pages contain the 17″ Nancy Ann dolls made during 1955 from a company brochure. They are excellent quality and highly collectable in their own right. But, you should be aware that some of these dolls have been sold as Alexanders. The "Queen" shown in Vol. 1 on page 103 is an example. It was shown in another doll book as being an Alexander doll, and many assumed that it was, including myself! The Nancy Ann Storybook Doll Company introduced a line 17″-18″ dolls that look a great deal like Madame Alexander dolls. This section shows a few that were on the market in 1952. Neither dolls, nor the clothes are tagged.

21″ "Nanette Teen" by Arranbee. All hard plastic, non-walker sleep blue eyes/lashes. Marks: R & B, on head. Elaborate brocade gown with satin lined jacket with real mink at sleeves. Square snaps. R & B doll hair differ from Alexanders in style, although this same "texture" was used on a few Alexander dolls, such as the Polly Pig-tail dolls. This was during the time when Alexander, Arranbee and American Character shared a common factory. The material of the gown on this doll is the same as used for part of the Alexander's "Fashion of the Century" series.

17″ 1953 hard plastic unmarked doll of good quality with thick strawberry blonde wig, with hair curled up and under (like an upward page boy-away from face and neck). Has blue sleep eyes/lashes with lashes painted under the eyes. Eyeshadow, teen-type flat feet with graceful arms and legs. Clothes are extra special from the beaded pearl and rhinestone crown that encircles the head to the beaded matching medalian on the pink shoulder sash. Underpants and matching hoop skirt are of printed white on white rayon satin. Pink nylons with built in garter tops to mid thigh. Pink flat satin shoes with ankle straps. Gown has heavy pink underskirt with real lace overdress in white with rhinestones scattered through out the skirt and around neck ruffle of lace. "Buttons" are pasted on chest to fill bodice. The original box polka-dot has original label that says: Style Show by Nancy Ann/"Her Royal Majesty, The Queen"/3401. Attached silver wrist card says the same thing on the gilt front. Back is empty, but inside are listed the following: #1501 "Summery Day/#1502 "Breath of Spring"/#1503 "Enchantment"/ #1504 "Lilac Time"/#1901 "Afternoon Tea"/#1902 "Heavenly Blue"/#1903 "Demure Miss"/#1904 "Garden Party"/#2401 "Moonlight Mist"/#2402 "Dinner Date"/#2403 "Sweet & Lovely"/#2404 "Sophistication"/#2901 "Grand Ball"/#2902 "Gay Evening"/#2903 "Opera Night"/#2904 "Wedding Night"/#3401 "Her Royal Majesty - The Queen". Clothes and doll are unmarked. Since the quality and the look of these dolls are very much "Alexander", errors can be made in their identity. (Courtesy Elizabeth Montesano of Yesterday's Children)

18″ Nancy Ann. All hard plastic with saran wig. Sleep eyes. Advertised in the 1953 FAO Schwarz catalog. This one is called "Old Fashioned Bouquet" doll and cost $29.95 in 1953. These dolls are listed as being "new" this year. This is a white embroidered nylon net dress over white taffeta. Four flower sprigs on skirt and one on each side of the part in her hair, encircled with a pale blue velvet ribbon. Carries a bouquet, and has long white pantalettes.

18″ Nancy Ann doll called "Lemon Froth" sold for $24.95 in 1953. Striped yellow sheer over yellow taffeta petticoat. High neckline and long sleeves trimmed with lemon colored velvet. Skirt has same velvet trim. Picture hat has lemon colored veiling and two large yellow roses for trim. Chignon styled coiffure.

18″ Nancy Ann doll called "Sapphire Blue". (Sold for $19.95 in 1953). Blue lace over pink taffeta, with narrow pink flowered braid trim. Wide pink satin ribbon sash at waist. Natural straw bonnet trimmed with same pink satin. Page boy hair style.

18″ Nancy Ann called "Lavender and Lace", sold for $15.95 in 1953. Organdy small floral design on lavender background with lace trimmed bodice. Natural straw hat.

Listed as "new" in the FAO Schwarz catalog of 1952 were four 18″ Nancy Ann dolls. This one is called "Her Royal Majesty" in white lace studded with rhinestones, over pink taffeta, pink satin ribbon with jewel ornament and crown of rhinestones and pearls. She sold for $34.95 in 1952.

18″ Nancy Ann doll that sold for $15.95 from the FAO Schwarz catalog of 1952. Called "Lilac Time", the doll is dressed in green striped taffeta with rolled brim straw hat trimmed with marabou.

This 18″ Nancy Ann doll of 1952 sold for $24.95 from the FAO Schwarz catalog. Called "Sweet and Lovely", she is dressed in full white net over pink taffeta with blue satin sash and trimmed with pink lilac.

In 1952 FAO Schwarz offered this 18″ Nancy Ann doll called "Heavenly Blue" for $19.95. The gown is powder blue taffeta with white lace and pink satin ribbon, natural straw bonnet trimmed with a large rose and ribbon.

17″ #1503 "White Lilacs" Nancy Ann all hard plastic doll of 1955. Gown is pale blue with flowers as are the sleeves. Blue bodice with white trim, matching trim at neck, sleeves and waist. Straw hat with blue ribbon and flowers.

17″ Nancy Ann all hard plastic #2902 "Forget Me Not". White/blue stripes on pink with black lace on skirt, cuffs and collar. Matching lace over straw hat with flowers.

17″ Nancy Ann hard plastic doll of 1955-#2401 "Gaiety". Blue striped gown with black lace/maroon trim and matching trim on bodice. Straw hat with flowers and wide maroon ribbon tie.

#1902 "Golden Gleam". 17″ all hard plastic and unmarked. Nancy Ann doll of 1955. Yellow satin full slip with pale yellow over-skirt with gold stars. Gold bodice with white lace trim. Tie on soft net stole and yellow flowers in hair.

17″ #1502 "Pinkie" by Nancy Ann. All hard plastic doll. Gown is entirely in pink with black picture hat and pink ribbon.

17″ Nancy Ann doll #1501 "Miss Checker Board". Blue/white check with red/white trim. Nancy hat with red flowers in material.

17″ #1901 "Miss Pinafore". All hard plastic with blue sleep eyes. Doll is unmarked. Gown is pink checked with white organdy pinafore, straw hat with flowers. Nancy Ann doll of 1955.

17″ Nancy Ann all hard plastic unmarked doll #1903 "Summer Afternoon". 1955. Gown is blue with white lace wide band around skirt and bunch of red flowers. Pink sash, picture straw hat with matching flowers.

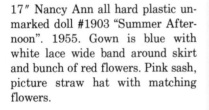

17″ Nancy Ann doll of 1955 #1904 "Sweet Miss." All pink gown with two rows white on skirt, white lace collar and cuffs and a matching pink bonnet that is material covered straw, tied with large pink ribbon.

17″ All hard plastic Nancy Ann #2404 "Lace Butterflies". Blue on blue stripes with lace on skirt, bodice and in hair.

17″ #2402 "Pink Pearl". Nancy Ann all hard plastic doll of 1955. Gown is silver grey with pink trim with pink flowers on hat.

17″ 1955 #2400 "Senior Prom". All pink with white lace overskirt, lace on bodice and cap. Red flowers.

17″ All hard plastic Nancy Ann #2903 "Dinner Dance". Blue with blue lace overlay on skirt and white fur jacket.

17″ #2904 "Bride". All hard plastic Nancy Ann in satin and white lace. Floor length veil with lace cap.

#2901 "Beautiful Lady". 17″ all hard plastic Nancy Ann dressed in lace pink with white fur jacket and pink flowers in hair.

17″ #1504 "Strawberry Festival". All hard plastic doll by Nancy Ann-1955. Pink dress covered with red strawberries. White bodice top and sleeves, red ribbon trim and ties. Straw hat with red feathers/trim.

18″ Nancy Ann with vinyl head and rooted hair. 1955. Shown in the FAO Schwarz catalog (sold for $15.95). This outfit is called "Pretty Pixie" and is a pink figured organdy over a pink taffeta petticoat. Sleeves and neck are trimmed with lace, skirt has ribbon sash. Ponytail hairdo.

This 18″ Nancy Ann doll was sold for $29.95 in the FAO Schwarz catalog of 1955. The gown is called "Moonbeam" and is blue nylon tulle over taffeta. Bodice is trimmed in silver and neckline with nylon tulle. Skirt is trimmed with shimmering silver braid.

ADDITIONS AND CORRECTIONS

It is quite impossible to compile a book on dolls that encompass over 50 years, and not make a mistake someplace. We have always tried to be the first to admit and correct our mistakes, and included in the following are these corrections. We have advertised and asked for help in spotting any errors in Volume I, so the following is also the combined efforts of many, and we give our thanks to them all.

One fact must be pointed out. . . variations did happen, colors varied, as did materials, and these "differences" are not to be mis-construed as making the doll what she was not intended to be. Companies are in business, and even if Madame Alexander always demanded (and got) the finest quality of workmanship and materials, "differences" did occur. For examples, the "name" tags may have run out and the standard "Madame Alexander" tag used, materials may have run out and different materials used for the same dress/doll, blue eyes (or brown) may have run short, so the brown (or blue) ones were used until a new supply came in. Madame Alexander has always made a "custom" built doll. . which means the dolls were made up AFTER the orders came in from the stores. This way of operating was a genius method on the part of Madame Alexander, as it eliminated left-over inventories and un-used stock, and may have played a very great part in her being able to continue making dolls when things were so very, very hard during the 1930's and 1940's.

It is suggested that you place the additions and errors into Volume I on the pages they belong. This will give you easy reference. Some take offense at writing in a book, but we see nothing but good in it; our own books are filled with notations and information, as we find it.

Page 4: Add under Tiny Betty: Oliver Twist, David Copperfield, Priscilla, Hiawatha, Jugo-slav, Brazlian, Princess Elizabeth, Nina Ballerina, Tiny Tim, Sonja Henie.

Page 4: Add under Little Betty: Nina Ballerina, Scarlett O'Hara, Sonja Henie, Swedish, Rubero & Rumbera of Cuba, Princess Elizabeth, Nina Ballerina, Tiny Tim, Sonja Henie, and American Indians.

Page 5: Add under Wendy Ann: Bride and trousseau, Chita (unknown), Godey, Judy, Marine and Miss America.

Page 5: Add under Princess Elizabeth: Nurse and Girl Scout.

Page 6: Add under Margaret O'Brien: Godey Bride, Godey Man, 20″ Godey, Good Fairy, Kathryn Grayson, Mommie and Me, Pink Bridesmaid, Pink Bride, Princess Elizabeth Bride (Royal Wedding).

Page 6: Add under Maggie: Arlene Dahl, Babs, John Powers, Goldilocks, Alice in Wonderland trousseau, Annabelle trousseau, Madelaine De Baines, Margot Ballerina.

Page 7: Add under Alexander-kins: Maggie Mix-up, Baby Wendy-kins, Little Madaline, Infant of Prague, trunks with wardrobes.

Page 8: Add under Cissy: trunks and wardrobes, Ice Capades, Binnie with wardrobe and trunk, Binnie Ballerina, Winnie with wardrobes and trunks.

Page 8: Add under Elise: Wardrobes and trunks.

Page 9: Add under Jacqueline: Ice Capades, wardrobes and trunks.

Page 9: Add to this page: Kelly (no photo): Mary-bel, Edith the Lonely Doll, Pollyanne, wardrobes and trunks.

Page 10: Rosie should be spelled Rozy.

Page 10: Add that Maria came before Polly, also add trunks and wardrobes for Polly.

Page 11: Add to dolls listed under Mary Ann: Discontinued dolls: Madame (1967-1975), Mary Ann (1965 only), Little Grannys' (1966), Orphant Annie (1956-1966), Riley's Little Annie (1967), Jenny Lind and cat (1969-1971), Jenny Lind (1970), Scarlett (1968), Renoir Girl, white dress (1967-1968), pink dress/pinafore (1969-1970) blue dress, Grandma Jane (1970), Peter Pan (1969), Wendy (1969), Snow White (Disney) (1977), Gidget (1966), McGuffey Ana (1968-1969), Rebecca with two-tiered skirt, Louisa, Liesl.

Page 11: There should be a separate "face" for the 12″ dolls, and they should be designated as the "Nancy Drew" face. Included would be the Pamela, Renoir Child, 12″ Little Women (other than Lissy), Pinkie, Blue Boy, Romeo and Juliet. Scratch Nancy Drew and Little Women from discription of Elise 17″.

Page 12: Add Pip from "Great Expectations" and Agnes from "David Copperfield".

Page 13: Louis instead of Lewis.

Page 14: 16″ Red Riding Hood.

Page 16: Change Little Shaver date from 1941 to 1942.

Page 17: Both Funny and Muffin were discontinued in 1978.

Page 18: Add: Many early Alexander boxes were yellow, covered with flowers. Add: to Tiny Betty 7″ to 8″ size: Oliver Twist 1935, David Copperfield 1935, Priscilla 1936-1939, Hiawatha 1936-1939, Jugo-slav 1939-1940, Brazilian 1937-1940, Princess Elizabeth 1937, Nina Ballerina 1936-1938. Change Bo Peep dates to 1937-1939, Chinese 1936 to 1940, Swedish 1936 to 1940, Hawaiian 1936-1940, Red Riding Hood 1936-1940, Alice In Wonderland 1935-1940, Belgium 1935-1939, Danish 1937-1940. 7″ Sonja Henie.

Page 18: Add: to Little Betty 9″-11″: Rumbero and Rumbera of Cuba 1939. Swiss should be Swedish. Nina Ballerina 1937-1939, Scarlett 1937-1939, Sonja Henie 1937-1940, Doll of Month Club dates are 1936-1940.

Page 18: Add: to Wendy Ann-11″, 12″, 13″, 14″: Ballerina 1936-1940, Fairy Princess 1940-1942, Sonja Henie.

Page 19: Add: 25″ and 27″ to Little Colonel 1935. Add to 1936: Dr. Defoe and nurse. Wendy Ann also came in 14″ size. Change Norman to Norma Shearer. Add to 1937: Princess Elizabeth-13″ has closed mouth (Little Colonel-Betty) Add: Carreen, played by Ann Rutherford has dark hair. Suellen played by Evelyn Keyes has reddish hair. Both also came in 17″ size. Add to Jane Withers: 17″ also came with cloth body. 19″ and 20″ also came with closed mouths. Add to Little Genius: Also came in 12″, 16″, 22″, 24″ and 27″ sizes. Add: Betty in 27″ size.

Page 20: 1938: Add Ballerina in 7″ and 11″ sizes. Add to 21″ Portraits-Chita (Unknown-Wendy).

Page 20: Flora McFlimsey: Scratch "from McGuffey Readers". Add: Based on W.A. Bulter's 1857 poem "Nothing To Wear".

Page 20: 1939: Add: Miss America. 1939 World's Fair and Freedom Train. Holds flag.

Page 22: 1941: Add hand puppet named Toby.

Page 22: 1942: Add Nurse in blue and white (Princess Elizabeth.

Page 23: 1946: Add Margaret O'Brien dressed for movie, "Meet Me In St. Louis" (1944) re-opened in New York-1946. Add: 21″ Portrait Godey. Add Alice In Wonderland (Margaret) in 17″ and 21″ sizes. Add: Judy (Wendy) 21″ from "Meet Me In St. Louis". Gown with pinch pleated flowers at hem, flowers in hair, wig rolled to top. To 1945 add: 21″ Portraits Victoria (Re-issue of Princess Flania) Melanie, Antoinette, Lady Windermere, Judy, Romance, Scarlett, Degas, Renoir, Godey.

Page 24: Add: Little Colonel tag not always as shown.

Page 25: 12″ Nurse may be an Effanbee doll (See MCD-Vol. 4).

Page 26: Change caption of 7″ David Copperfield to read "Courtesy Jane Thomas".

Page 27: "It" dolls were made by Amberg & Sons. The ones purchased by Alexander did not have a jointed (ball) waist.

Page 28: Change spelling to Dr. Defoe (all one word).

Page 32: There have been three Superior companies. The one based in New York went out of business in 1922. One American company by this name remains: Superior Toy & Mfg. Co. of Chicago.

Page 33: Change caption of 7″ Red Riding Hood to "Courtesy Glorya Woods".

Page 33: "Pollera" is actually name of garment.

Page 36: Change caption of 7″ Hansel to "Courtesy Mary Ann Keepers".

Page 42: There is no information on the doll sitting with Jane Withers. The photo does help us date these dolls.

Page 46: Change 9″ Dilly Dally Sally to "Courtesy Mary Ann Keepers".

Page 55: 21″ Scarlett dressed by Laural Dicicco.

Page 59: Change 7″ Fairy Princess to "Courtesy Helen M. Bohler".

Page 62: Scarletts. Some may have come with blue, instead of green eyes, due to production shortages. After newness of movie, the dolls name was changed to "Southern Girl" and may have either blue or green eyes.

Page 75: Add notation: Collectors measure a doll from the top of the forehead to the sole of the feet, and manufacturers measure from the center, of the top of the head, to the sole of the feet. Because of the different methods of measuring there is usually 1″ less to the collectors measure as there is to the manufactures measure.

Page 75: 1948: Add Old Fashioned Girl came in 14″ and 17″ sizes and was made for FAO Schwarz. Add: 14″ and 17″ Madeliene de Baines (Maggie). Add: 21″ Portraits. Group unknown except Godey Lady.

Page 76: 14″ Beth: Since Beth is generally a brunette, this may be a Meg and 15″ Meg may be a Jo (dress and doll).

Page 77: Change Little Genius from 1″ to 21″. Typographical error: 14″ Lucy Bride: word ending third sentence should be "not".

Page 77: Add: 14″ Madeliene de Baines (Maggie) FAO Schwarz. Add: Babs-non-skater (Maggie & Margaret) Add: Margot Ballerina (Maggie).

Page 79: Typographical error: 17″ Lucy Bride. Last word should be "veil".

Page 81: 1950: Add 17″ & 21″ Mary Martin. Babs Skater (Margaret & Maggie). 18″ Prince Charming. Pink gown to 14″, 17″ & 21″ Bride. Add: 20″ Kathryn Grayson (Margaret). 20″ Arlene Dahl (Maggie). Teenager to Maggie Walker (also came with wardrobe). Add to Divine-a-lite: Sunbeam came with painted eyes that are half-closed. (Had a-sleep eyes in 1951). Add: 14″ Godey Group. Add: 14″ Ring-Bearer with Lovey-Dovey head.

Page 82: Change 14″ Mary Martin to "South Pacific".

Page 83: Babs and Babsie came dressed in different outfits, as well as in skate costume.

Page 84: 21″ Maggie's dress may be on backward.

Page 85: Lovey Dovey came on various body styles, such as all hard plastic, laytex and all vinyl.

Page 85: 1951: Add: 21″ McGuffey Ana (Margaret). 18″ Goldilocks (Maggie) for Nieman Markus. 15½″-16″ Looby Loo. Add: Margot Ballerina in 14″ and 18″.

Page 86: 1951: Add: 20″ Godey group. 12″ Bonnie with one-piece laytex body and limbs.

Page 87: Change 25″ Maggie Walker to Binnie Walker. 18″ Violet to Courtesy Carrie Perkins.

Page 88: 18″ "Alice" was not meant to be an Alice in Wonderland. 17″ Kathy may be a Maggie, as Kathy seems to always have had braided hair.

Page 89: 14″ Marme has replaced lace. 14″ Jo. Some of the large hand dolls were used up to 1955.

Page 91: 1952: Add: 14″, 17″ & 20″ Kathy (Maggie). Change "Little Women" from 15″ to 14″. add 21″ to Snow White.

Page 92: Add 14″ to John Powers Models. 13″ Treena Ballerina, change Margaret to Maggie.

Page 93: Change 20″ Annabelle to Kathy (Braids).

Page 94: 14½″ Maggie Walker is #1511.

Page 95: 15″ Snow White is #1535, 18″ is #1835 and 23″ is #2335.

Page 98: 1953: Add: 14″ Mommie & Me (Margaret) Walker. Matching 7½″-8″. Add Maggie to Margot Ballerina.

Page 99: 1953: Change Queen Elizabeth to 20″. Add Wendy Ann/Alexander-kins, Billy also sold in trunks and cases. Add 7½″ Little Madaline with dresses same as large one.

Page 100: Change Prince Phillip and Queen to Lord Admiral and Lady.

Page 101: Add 14″ to Choir boys.

Page 103: 17″ Queen Mother is a Nancy Ann Storybook doll. See the Comparison study and the Nancy Ann section in the black and white section.

Page 106: Change 8″ Agatha to "Courtesy Mable Sherman", 8″ Peter Pan to Courtesy Daisy Houghtaling, 8″ Little Southern Girl Courtesy Jane Thomas.

Page 109: 1954: Add Mommie and Me, repeat from 1953. Add Flowergirl (Margaret), Bonnie also in 12″ size. Add to Alexander-kins: Also came with one piece vinyl body and limbs. Add 12″ Little Audrey (Lovey Dovey) with one-piece body and limbs and molded hair under wig.

Page 110: 1954: Add Alexander-kins also offered in trunks and cases.

Page 111: 18″ Civil War, change to #2101-1953.

Page 112: Change 8″ Little Southern Girl to "Courtesy Mable Sherman", 8″ Apple Annie to "Courtesy Mable Sherman", 8″ Victoria "Courtesy Jane Thomas".

Page 113: 8″ Bill: Change bend knees to straight legs. Change Wendy Ann #393 to jacket instead of coat.

Page 114: 8″ "Billie" is actually a doll made after 1973, but the sleeper is 1954..

Page 115: 13″ Dryer Baby: Scratch line, "See following photo, etc.". 14″ hard plastic is an Arranbee doll (Nanette) is an Alexander outfit.

Page 116: 15″ Meg: There were several variations of flowered prints used.

Page 119: 1955: 20″ Cissy may have a replaced hat.

Page 122: 1955: Add 8″ Cinderella #492 and change "Courtesy Phyllis DeMent". Add 8″ Little Godey #491 and change "Courtesy Phyllis DeMent". Add 8″ Alice in Wonderland #465 and change "Courtesy Ann Tuma". Change 8″ Wendy Ann #457 to bend knee.

Page 123: Add to Dude Ranch #449.

Page 124: Change 8″ Wendy from #445 to #448.

Page 125: Change Wendy from #449 to #439.

Page 126: Change Wendy from #464 to #458.

Page 127: 1956: Change Story Princess from Margaret to Cissy. Add Lissy Graduate (with diploma).

Page 128: 1956: Add 8″ Easter Bunny, holding basket and in larger eggs. Change caption under Cissy #2096 to page 129 and Cissy #2020.

Page 129: Change Cissy #2014 to "red belt" instead of vest. Change caption under Cissy #2020 to page 128 under Cissy #2096.

Page 131: Change Cousin Karen to "Courtesy Jane Thomas".

Page 133: Change 8″ Wendy #556 to #554.

Page 134: Change Wendy #346 to #546.

Page 135: Change Wendy #538 to #518 (also had variations of print used for this dress). Change Wendy #538 to #548.

Page 136: Change Wendy #584 to #592. Change Wendy #554 to #564.

Page 137: Change Wendy #555 to #558.

Page 138: 12″ Lissy is actually a Pamela and should not be shown on this page (Also on page 227).

Page 140: 21″ Scarlett-1962 was used again in 1965 as Godey. Catalog shows a blonde, with white lace inside bonnet. The 21″ Queen is actually #2185-1968. The 1965 Queen is in gold brocade gown with gold roses.

Page 148: Change 11″ Jenny Lind to #1184-1970 (with lace), other shown on page 280 (without lace-#1171-1969).

Page 151: Change Wendy Ann Does the Mombo to "Courtesy Carrie Perkins".

Page 173: 1957: Add 21″ Princess Grace (Cissy). Gold filagree gown with gold lame half bodice and sleeves.

Page 177: 12″ Meg may be a Beth.

Page 179: Change 10″ Cissette #973 to #977.

Page 180: Change 10″ Cissette #805-1957 to #805-1958.

Page 181: Change Cissette #0924 to #0923.

Page 182: Change Cissette #910 to #915.

Page 187: Change 9″ Bitsey and Butch to 1967.

Page 188: Change 8″ Wendy from #366 to #374.

Page 191: Add: 16½″ Elise (pants and navy jacket) #1720-1958.

Page 196: Add to 15″ Kathy Tears: #3910-1959. Add Kelly also came in an 8″ size. Add Sleeping Beauty also came in an 18″ size.

Page 199: Change 30″ Betty to 1960.

Page 201: "Disney" Cissettes have flat feet.

Page 206: Add following 21″ Portraits to Scarlett, Melanie and Queen Elizabeth: Godey in orange (Cissy), Renoir in yellow (Cissy) and Lissy in pink (Cissy). Add 8″ Lissy Americana (Per 12″ Lissy).

Page 211: Add to Faith #486, and change to "Courtesy Jane Thomas". Change Amanda to "Courtesy Jane Thomas".

Page 215: 1962: Add Elise came this one year with a bouffant hair-style. Add: somali leopard or mink fur coats, styled by Andre Fath of Paris at $400.00 each were available for Jacqueline.

Page 217: Some of the FAO Schwarz and Marshall Field doll/trunks were made up by them, and not by the Alexander Co., therefore some of these outfits will be tagged "Alexander". The 21″ Jackie clothes (except what she is wearing) is tagged: Petite Fashions by Debutant.

Page 221: Change 8″ Scots Lass to "Courtesy Jane Thomas".

Page 222: Add 18″ Mama Kitten #9069-1963.

Page 223: 17″ Elise Ballerina has the Marybel head used the last year of the older Elise production.

Page 224: 1963. Add: 20″ Melinda (Kelly/Mary-bel) with length hair, in trunk for Marshall Field. Add: Elise Bride 14″ & 18″.

Page 226: 12″ Lissy Alice in Wonderland: this outfit also used in Pamela case.

Page 227: 12″ Pamela dressed in outfit also made for Lissy. Change to "Courtesy Carrie Perkins". 12″ Smarty is in a 1965 Janie ballerina outfit.

Page 230: 15″: Change Honey Bea to Sugar Tears 1965. Honey Bea/Sugar Tears are marked 1962 and have swivel joints. Most 16″ Sugar Tears of 1965 have flange joints.

Page 233: 12″ Beth doll may be a McGuffey Ana as Beth not usually a pigtail blonde. She has on the wrong pinafore. The pinafore goes with Lissy outfit #1240-1956.

Page 236: Change spelling to Fischer Quints.

Page 237: Change spelling to Binnie.

Page 237: 1965: Add Yolanda should be a blonde, but more have been found that were redheads, than blonde. There has also been tagged, in the box, Brenda Starrs with blonde hair.

Page 237: Change 17″ Maria to Polly and Elise. Change Baby Ellen to 14″ size only. Add: Mary-bel came in case with long, straight blonde hair.

Page 238: Add: Mary Ellen Playmate 14″ (Mary Ann) for Wanamakers.

Page 239: Change Louise to Louisa, Brigetta to Brigitta, Fredrick to Friedrich. Gretel to Gretl and Liesl to Leisl. Add: 13″ Leisl has orange dress under green striped apron.

Page 240: 12″ Pamela: change velour to velcro.

Page 242: Blonde/bangs Mary Ellen Playmate in blue polka dot dress/matching shoes also sold by Marshall Field (17″).

Page 249: 1966: 14″, 20″ and 24″ Lively Pussy Cat discontinued after one year.

Page 249: Add: Mary Ellen Playmate for Marshall Field is 14″ (Mary Ann) in red cotton dress with 2 rows white eyelet trim around hem and sleeves. Red side snap shoes. Dark hair in braids and full bangs.

Page 251: 14″ Granny #1431 should have glasses.

Page 257: 18″ Victoria has replaced clothes.

Page 258: 1967: Add 17″ Queen #1790 (Elise).

Page 259: Renoir Dolls inspired from paintings by Pierre Renoir.

Page 263: Add Disney Crest colors on Snow White: Gold Skirt/black bodice/rose res cape/gold trim/white collar and ribbon. Add: 14″ Riley's Little Annie: olive green green leaves, pink flowers on white. Pink hat with green ribbon and white flowers.

Page 264: Change 14″ Madame to Revolution Era.

Page 269: 1968: 14″ Rebecca is actually a 1970 doll. 1968 and 1969 has no lace around hem and skirt is in two tiers.

Page 273: Add: 20″ Rusty used the Pussy Cat body in 1967, Puddin' body in 1968 with same heads, but clothes different for the two years.

Page 278: Add: Bride Elise was used on the cover of the June issue of McCalls. 1969.

Page 280: Add: 14″ inspired by book by Frances Cavanah "Jenny Lind & Her Listening Cat".

Page 282: Add: 1969: Michael's bear was made by Shuco.

Page 284: Change gowns for 14″ dolls from Elise to Mary Ann. Add 22″ So Big. Made last under that name in 1975. Mold continued being used for "Pumpkin with wig".

Page 285: Add Victoria had cloth feet only during 1966, after that she had vinyl lower legs.

Page 289: Change 8″ Red Boy from 1970 to 1972 (first issued in 1972).

Page 289: Red Boy from the Francisco de Goya's painting of young prime minister of Spain (to Queen Luisa). Priscilla from Henry Wadsworth Long-fellow's poem "Courtship of Miles Standish" of Priscilla and John Alden (as proxy for Miles Standish).

Page 292: Add: Louisa is missing from "Sound of Music" set.

Page 297: 14″ Renoir Child: Later ones do not have straw hats ("1478).

Page 297: 10″ Queen also came with brown eyes and hair.

Page 301: Change: 9″ Sweet Tears discontinued in 1975.

Page 303: Pinkie from Joshua Reynolds (1723-1792) painting. Blue Boy from painting by Thomas Gainsborough (1727-1788).

Page 305: Add: Some 1976 Portraits are mis-tagged-Agatha for Cornelia and vise versa. Add: the 14″ Baby Precious in the 14″ was made one year only (1975), and discontinued in 1976. Add: As of 1976 the 8″ dolls are now marked "Alexander" and not just "Alex." Add: 14″ and 21″ Rosey Posey - made this one year only (1976).

Page 306: Add these "faces" to First Ladies: Martha Washington has new face, and others like her will be designated as (Martha). Abigail Adams-Mary Ann, Martha, Randolph-Elise, Dolly Madison-new Martha face, Elizabeth Monroe-Mary Ann, Louisa Adams-Elise.

Page 309: Add: Baby Lynn came in 20″ only and discontinued in 1977. Add: 17″ Baby McGuffey discontinued. 19″-20″ Baby Precious discontinued and 14″ size made one year and discontinued (1977). Elise in formal 17″ discontinued. 14″ Black and 24″ Pussy Cat (white) discontinued.

Page 310: Add: Baby Brother (1977) and now Sister (1979) are Puddin' with mold changes. Add: 20″ Mommie's Pet is new for Baby Lynn.

Page 311: Change 14″ and 21″ Mary Mine to Rosey-Posey/Puddin' with mold change).

It was in the March 1964 Playthings magazine that the following was reported:

"Madame Alexander . . is branching out. It is reported that her collection of infants' and children's wear will be in the New York stores soon . . . under the name of Madame Alexander Tots, Inc.

The clothing samples are said by those who have seen them to be typical Madame Alexander creations . . . flawlessly designed. Madame Alexander states that her entry into the infants' and children's wear field was prompted by the many letters asking, "Why can't children look like your dolls?"

The result is Madame Alexander designed clothes for "midgies", petti-tots and toddlers. These will be sold along with the lady's world renowned dolls at FAO Schwarz. In addition, Madame Alexander has designed a series of doll costumes corresponding in styling and appearance to the infant's and children's apparel."

Someplace there are clothes for infants and children that bear the Madame Alexander tag, and it will be fun to see if any survived to fall into the hands of a collector. It would especially be fun to find one of the outfits that was also designed for a doll, as well as for the infant or child.

CISSETTE

Cissette is a difficult doll to date (if nude) and here are a few ways that may help: from 1957 to 1958 the wigs had three rows of stitching, and in 1959 through 1963 the stitches were zig-zag. From 1957 into 1960 there was no fingernail polish, and from 1960's to 1963, the fingernails were polished. In 1957 the eyelids were beige and 1958 they were pale pink, all other years were pink (except as Margot/Portrettes, which were blue . . . also Jacqueline). Bodice darts were used from 1957 to 1959 on all Cissette clothes and from 1960 to 1963, no darts were used except in formal wear. Cissette tags should all be turquoise, except in 1963 when they were blue.

WRIST TAGS

Wrist tags: Mid 1930's to mid-1940's: gold cardboard octagonal tags with name of doll (there are exceptions) on one side and the company name on the other. Mid 1940's into 1951: green or gold metallic cloverleaf with company name on one side and sometimes (not too often) name of doll on other side. Square metallic silver tag from 1950 into 1953 (non-Fashion Award). 1951 into 1954: gold metal, necklace or tag of the Fashion Academy Award.

CLOTHES

Early cloth dolls clothes were pinned, never sewn on. The early compositions can come with clothes pinned, also, but never stapled on. Square snaps were used by many manufacturers (American Character, Arranbee, etc.). Alexander also used button holes and ties, but never the slide snaps such as Vogue "Ginny" clothes did.

WENDY and WENDY ANN

7½" and 8" Alexander-kins/Wendy and Wendy Ann dolls are marked ALEX., on the back except on the dolls made AFTER 1976, and these are marked with the full ALEXANDER, on the backs. Dress tags generally will read: (in green, blue or red) Alexander-kins/by Madame Alexander/Reg. U.S. Pat. Off. N.Y.,N.Y., or Alexander-kins . . .followed by name of doll . ./Reg. U.S. Pat. Off. N.Y., N.Y., a few will be tagged: Madame Alexander/All Rights Reserved New York, U.S.A.

NEW DOLLS FOR 1980 ARE:

Four 12" ones: Cleopatra, Mark Anthony, Josephine and Napolean. These are a continuation of "Great Lovers" series that include: Pinky and Blue Boy and Romeo and Juliet. The Largest Little Brother and Sister are the only ones discontinued.

American Home 52:50-1 Ja'54

Arts & Decorations 40:54-5 Ap, '34

Business Women: 61-3, D 24 '66

Consumer Rep. 32: 56, 6 N'67

Coronet 25:110-14 D'48

Dolls in Books, M.L. Morris

Goldilocks, M.A. McDowell: st n '64 & 29 N'36

Good Housekeeping 141:201-4 & D'55

Horn 30:8 F'54

Independent Women 19:390 D'40

Life 28:75 Ap 10'50 & 102-3 D-'9 '40 & 33, 83 & 52 2'52

Look 18:102-4 & N 16 '54

Louisa May Alcott: Reminisencies by the Original.

New York Times: Ap2, 23:2 '35, Ap 24, 7:5 '35, My 29, 23:5 '35, 0 29, 23:3 '35, D 22, 11, 12:1 '35, D28, 13:8 '35, P 56-7 D 12'48, P 34, My 26'53, P 19 N 3'57, Ja 3-17:6 to Ja 5, 11-6:5 '36, 0 27, 27:4-026, 19:5 '36, N20, 11:3 ed, N 21, 16:4 '36, D7, 42:3 '36, D 11, 41:5 '36, D 13, V111, P.8 '36, 025, 21:8-0 26, 25:2 '37, N 18, 42:6-'37, Ap. 23, 32:1 '38, Ap 26, 23:2 '38, 025, 25:5 '38, N 2, 41:6 '38, F28, 36:1 '39, Myl, 38:4 '39, 031, 25:2 '39, N 4, 29; & '39, D17, V11, P.8 '39, Je20, 25:6 '40, S 6, 11:2 '40, 022, 20:7 '40, 023, 34:7 '40, D11, 34:3 '40, Ap 26, 17:5 '41, D 28, 11, 7, 6, '41, Ap 7, 25:2 '42, My 7, 15:3 '42, N 12, 26:2 '43, F 18, 19:3 '44, N6, 22:4 '44, N7, 30:4 '44, F27, 8:5 '45, D 25, 29:4 '45, Mr 12, 27:2 '46, My 2, 18:1 '46, My 12 V1, P 40 '46, S 27, 17:2 '46, Ap 3 27:3 '47, N 4, 30:3 '47, 0 27, 5:6 '48 Ag 21, 71:3 & Ag 24, 31:1 '49, 0 18, 32:4 '49

New Yorker: 26:18 Ag. 12 '50

Newsweek: 65:92 F 22'65, 56:85 6D5'60

Parents Mag: 26:184-5 0'51, 31:24 J 1 '56

Playbill: P 15, Mr 30 '53

Popular Science: 133:90-3 0'38

Sch. Arts. 37:106 D'37, 44:251 Mr '45, 48:51 0'48

Women's Home: C78:74 5 Ja'51

Jacobsen, Carole: Portrait of Dolls, Vol. I, II, III

Cooper, Marlowe: Doll Home Library Series Vol. 12, 13 & 14

Shoemaker, Rhonda: Price Guide for Madame Alexander Dolls, 1975-1977

Watson, Ellie: Wee Friends, 1974, Vol. II-1977

Thomas, Jane: The Most Beautiful Dolls

Foulke, Jan: Focusing on Oct. 1976 Doll Reader, other Doll Reader articles, Blue Book of Doll Values, Vol. 1, 2 & 3, Focusing on: Treasury of Mme. Alexander Dolls

Martinez, M.: Alexander Company brochures and catalogs and bills of lading 1934 to 1965

McKeon, Barbara Jo: Rare and Hard to Find Madame Alexander dolls.

Burdick, Lorraine: Celebrity Doll Journel: May, Aug: 1976, Aug. 1975, Adult Star Dolls & Toys 1973, Child Star Dolls & Toys 1968.

Alexander Catalog reprints (Jane Thomas) 1942-1952 to 1977

Taylor Deems. A Pictorial History of the Movies. 1943.

Springer & Hamilton. They Had Faces Then. 1974

Shipman, David. The Great Movie Stars. 1973

Settel & Laas. A Pictorial History of Television. 1969

Scheuer, Steven. The Movie Book. 1974

Likeness, George. The Oscar People. 1965

Time Inc. Life Goes To The Movies. 1975

Flamini, Roland. Scarlett, Rhett and a Cast of Thousands. 1975

Biggs, Marjorie. Madame Alexander "Little People".

Bexton & Owen. Radio's Golden Age. 1966

Brown, Vivian, Canton Repository: Tues. Mar. 11, 1975

Photoplay Treasury. 1975

Eames, John. The MGM Story. 1977

Town and Country. May 1964

Screen Guild. Oct. 1939

Toy Trader: May '55, May, June, July, Oct. 1964, Mar. May, June, July, Dec. 1965, April, June, July 1966, Jan. 1967

Doll News: (U.F.D.C.) Aug. 1970

The Family Circle: Sept., Nov. 1942, May 1943, Feb. 1944.

Consumer Reporter. Nov. 1967

McCalls. Nov. 1954, June 1956, Aug. 1957

Good Housekeeping. Nov. 1937, Dec. 1937, Nov. & Dec. 1938

Child Life. Dec. 1938, Jan. 1939, Dec. 1940

Plaything Mag. Jan. 1936 to July 1979

Library Bibliography of 1954, 1955, 1956, 1957 and 1958

Wonderful World of Toys From Disneyland. 1960

South Florida Today. Jan. 1976

New York Herald Tribune. May 26, 1963

Palm Beach Post. Apr. 1, 1976

Montgomery Wards. 1935, 1936, 1937, 1938, 1939, 1940-1970

FAO Schwarz. 1939, 1940, 1947-1972

Marshall Field. 1953-1968, 1969

Nieman Marcus. 1950's

J.E. Vincent: K.C. Star. 1930-1958

John Plain. 1940-1951

Sears Roebuck. 1935-1970

Abrahm-Strauss. 1950's

Wanamakers. 1948, 1950, 1956

Playthings Mag. 1945-1979

INDEX

Persons names are arranged with last name first, but dolls are first names first (Brenda Starr, Jane Withers, etc.)